KB090434

You're Hired!

Resume & Letter Writing
for English Language Learners

Myeong-hee Seong
Katie Mae Klemsen

BAEKSAN
Publishing Co.

Δverview

Form and Function	• The True Purpose of a Resume • The Most Internationally Competitive Resume Layouts • How to Be Remembered
The SEEK Approach	• How to Write a Balanced Resume • The Best Way to Remember the Most Important Components • How to Look Your Best on Paper
Writing for Resumes	• How to Write Job Descriptions • How to Create a Summary of Qualifications • The 3 Rs of Resume Writing
Contents	• What to Include and What Not to Include • The Art of Powerwords • How to Extract Skills from Experiences
Resume Etiquette	• Where to Put References • Understanding When to Phase-Out • How to Get Your Resume Read
Letters	• The Most Current Cover Letters and Business Letters • The 7 Rules of Thank you • Letter Opening and Closing Strategies

C·o·n·t·e·n·t·s

C·o·n·t·e·n·t·s

1 UNIT

First Things First

You're Hired!

Unit 1   First Things First

✎ Concepts

- Create a basic cover letter
- Learn the concepts of each section
- Reinforce resume and interview vocabulary

Vocabulary

- Announcements
- Innovative
- Naïve
- Opportunity
- Personalized
- Specialist
- To obtain
- Distinct
- Representatives
- Enclosure

- Job hunting
- Documents
- First impression
- Qualifications
- To make aware
- Skill set
- Varying
- Solutions
- Consideration
- Ability

Let's Get Started

Conversation I

1. Listen to the conversation between the two speakers. What issue is being discussed?

Madison:	Hi, Brian. How are you?
Brian:	I am well, thanks. What are you up to?
Madison:	Just looking at some job announcements. I've been job hunting for some time now, and I think I have found the perfect job.
Brian:	Really? That's great news, Madison. What is it?
Madison:	It's for a medical equipment company. They create innovative products for hospitals and clinics.
Brian:	Wow, that does sound like the perfect job for you.
Madison:	I told you. All I have to do is send a cover letter, resume, and two letters of reference.
Brian:	I see. Do you have those documents already?
Madison:	No. But really, how hard could it be?
Brian:	Madison, don't be naïve. It could be harder than it looks.
Madison:	What do you suggest I do then? I can't miss this opportunity!
Brian:	I can help you. Let's start by doing some research on cover letters. They are the first impression a company has of you. It's got to be good.

2. Listen again, and fill in the missing parts of speech.

Madison: Hi, Brian. How are you?

Brian: I am well, (1) _____. What are you up to?

Madison: Just (2) _____ at some job announcements. I've been job-hunting for some time now, and I think I have found the (3) _____ job.

Brian: Really? That's great news, Madison. What is it?

Madison: It's for a (4) _____ equipment company. They create innovative products for hospitals and clinics.

Brian: Wow, that does sound like the (5) _____ job for you.

Madison: I told you. All I have to do is send a cover letter, resume, and two letters of reference.

Brian: I see. Do you have those (6) _____ already?

Madison: No. But really, how hard could it be?

Brian: Madison, don't be naïve. It could be (7) _____ than it looks.

Madison: What do you suggest I do then? I can't miss this (8) _____!

Brian: I can help you. Let's start by doing some (9) _____ on cover letters. They are the first impression a company has of you. It's got to be good.

Conversation Ⅱ

1. Listen to the conversation between the two speakers. What information has been listed about making a great cover letter?

Brian: Look at this! This is a clear description of a cover letter.

Madison: It says that a cover letter should be a short introduction of yourself, details about the exact job you are applying for, and why you are qualified.

Brian: It also says that a cover letter is a formal letter and should be written as such.

Madison: That's right. It's not the same as writing a letter to your grandmother.

Brian: It also says that it should be personalized for each individual job and with the name of the company and person receiving the letter.

Madison: That must be so they know that I have taken time to write an individual letter. It shows the job is important to me.

Brian: Excellent, Madison, let's get started.

Brian: (1) _____! This is a clear description of a cover letter.

Madison: It says that a cover letter should be (2) _____, details about the exact job you are applying for, and why you are qualified.

Brian: It also says that (3) _____ and should be written as such.

Madison: That's right. It's not the same as writing a letter to your grandmother.

Brian: It also says that (4) _____ for each individual job and with the name of the company and person receiving the letter.

Madison: That must be so they know that I have taken time to write an individual letter. It shows the job is important to me.

Brian: Excellent, Madison, (5) _____.

Let's Get to Business

Cover Letter Sample I

Madison Klemsen
140 Kristi Court
Oregon City, Oregon
97045
(503) 810-3160

December 2, 2009

To Dr. Sean H. Kim:

I am eager to apply for the position of Lead Social Service Specialist. I was made aware of this exciting employment opportunity by an employment posting in the Korea Express newspaper.

During my academic experience, I have attained the skill set required to be successful in this work. I am committed to service and diligent work. I am dedicated to raising the quality of life for all individuals. This would be a great asset as a social service specialist.

I am confident in my skills and abilities to represent Human Solutions for several reasons. I have taken courses in educational programs and policies. I possess a very proficient understanding of the needs assessment processes. I speak, read and write fluent Korean and English. I have spent several years in Korea, as well as Japan and possess an in-depth understanding of the varying and distinct customs and cultures. This will help provide support for the diverse community of Oregon City.

I have obtained a very profound understanding of why and how poverty occurs. Also, I have been a part of teams that created sustainable, holistic and empowering solutions for this global pandemic. My university education, as well as personal experience has prepared me to begin my career.

Please review my enclosed resume for further consideration of an employment opportunity. I would appreciate an opportunity to further discuss my skills and qualifications with you or one of your representatives. Thank you for your attention.

Sincerely,
Madison Klemsen
Madison Klemsen

Enclosure: Resume

Cover Letter Template

Your Name
Address line 1
Address line 2
Address line 3
Phone number

Date

Name of recipient:

This is where you tell the reader which job you are applying for and where you gained knowledge of the job opening. If a friend or current company employee referred you, this is the perfect place to tell the reader. It lets them know more about who you are and whom you are connected to. Networking is important, so use it here.

In this section list the reasons, in a graduated and logical manner, why you are qualified for this position. Which skills do you have? What courses have you taken? What knowledge do you possess? Are you certified in something? Highlight your best professional and academic qualities.

This is a second paragraph regarding skills, knowledge and abilities. This can include personal experiences, related to professional, intern or academic experiences that will help the reader get to know you. Create a clear understanding of who you are.

This is your final paragraph. It is a closing statement asking the reader to review your resume, and consider you for the job. This is also a great place to invite the reader to call you to schedule an interview. Thank the reader for their time and attention.

Sincerely,
Signature
Your name

Enclosure: Resume

Practice Makes Perfect

Write Your Own

Complete the Text

Madison Klemsen
140 (1)_____ Court
Oregon City, Oregon
97045
(503) 810-3160

(2)_____ 2, 2009

To Dr. Sean H. Kim:

I am (3)_____ to apply for the position of Lead Social Service
Specialist. I was made aware of this (4)_____ (5)_____
(6)_____ by an employment posting in the Korea Express
newspaper.

During my academic experience, I have attained the (7)_____
(8)_____ required to be (9)_____ in this work. I am
committed to service and diligent work. I am dedicated to raising the
quality of life for all individuals. This would be a great (10)_____
as a social service specialist.

I am confident in my skills and (11)_____ to (12)_____ Human Solutions for several reasons. I have taken courses in educational programs and policies. I possess a very (13)_____ understanding of the needs assessment processes. I speak, read and write fluent Korean and English. I have spent several years in Korea, as well as Japan and possess an in-depth understanding of the (14)_____ and (15)_____ customs and cultures. This will help provide support for the diverse community of Oregon City.

I have obtained a very (16)_____ understanding of why and how poverty occurs. Also, I have been a part of teams that created sustainable, holistic and empowering solutions for this global pandemic. My university education, as well as personal experience has prepared me to begin my career.

Please review my (17)_____ resume for further consideration of an employment (18)_____. I would appreciate an opportunity to further discuss my skills and qualifications with you or one of your representatives. Thank you for your attention.

(19) _____,

Madison Klemsen
Madison Klemsen

Enclosure: (20) _____

Expressions

Letters begin with an opening phrase, usually directly addressing the reader. This first line sets the tone of the letter. A comma follows most opening phrases, however a colon follows others. An opening phrase from the formal list is the best choice.

> It is considered unacceptable, and far too personal, to select an opening phrase from the informal or casual / intimate list. Please only consider the use of formal opening phrases for cover letters, business letters and e-mails.

1. Review the following sample of an opening phrase.

Dear Mr. Kim,

2. Review the following opening phrases.

Formal
- Dear,
- To Whom It May Concern:
- Mr. _____,
- Mrs. _____,
- Ms. _____,
- Dear Sir:
- Dear Madam:

Informal
- My dear _____,
- Dearest _____,

Casual / Intimate
- My very dearest _____,
- Dear sweet _____,

How-To Tip

Writing the address on an envelope in English can be tricky. Order is important. It is also important to understand what each part of the address represents. Follow the guide below for perfect envelopes, every time.

1. Review the envelope template below.

Your name
Your home / office
Your city, your state
Your city zip code
Your country

> Receiver name
> Receiver title
> Receiver office / home address
> Receiver city, state
> State zip code
> COUNTRY in CAPS

2. Review the following sample of an envelope being sent to a US address.

Madison Klemsen
140 Kristi Court
Oregon City, Oregon
97045
USA

> Jeremy Brooks
> 1980 26[th]Street
> June, Oregon
> 97045
> USA

Concepts

Answer the following questions about cover letters.

1) What is the main topic of the first paragraph of a cover letter?

2) What is the purpose of a cover letter?

3) Why should you include the name of the company you are applying for?

4) Whose name should you include, other than your own, in a cover letter?

5) What information is included in the third and fourth paragraphs of a cover letter?

Wanted: Experience

You're Hired!

Unit 2 Wanted: Experience

✏️ Concepts

- Create a cover letter for an internship
- Learn how a basic cover letter is different from one to solicit an internship
- Reinforce resume and interview vocabulary

Vocabulary

- To finalize
- To tailor
- Master degree
- Policy
- To establish
- Regards
- Affectionately
- Academic
- Unpaid
- To expect

- Internship
- Bachelor degree
- Background
- Assistant
- Schedule
- Cordially
- To solicit
- Program
- To wrap up
- Intervention

Let's Get Started

Conversation Ⅰ

1. Listen to the conversation between the two speakers. What issue is being discussed?

Won-shin:	Hey, Ji-eun. How is your semester wrapping up?
Ji-eun:	It's going well. I am finalizing my plans for an internship, and studying for final exams.
Won-shin:	You're ahead of me. I am not sure how to find an internship.
Ji-eun:	It's not so hard, Won-shin. Do you have your cover letter and resume ready to send out?
Won-shin:	I have those documents, but they are not suitable for soliciting an internship. What can I do?
Ji-eun:	I just made a few changes to my basic documents, and that was it.
Won-shin:	Well, if that is all I have to do, then I might be more prepared than I thought.
Ji-eun:	Yea, the hard part is over. You just need to tailor the cover letter.
Won-shin:	Well, I am still not sure where to begin. Do you mind giving me a hand?
Ji-eun:	Sure thing. That is the least I can do for a friend.
Won-shin:	Thanks. And when I get the internship of my dreams, I will have you to thank.

Won-shin:　Hey, Ji-eun. How is your (1) _____ wrapping up?

Ji-eun:　It's going well. I am finalizing my plans for an (2) _____, and studying for final exams.

Won-shin:　You're ahead of me. I am not sure how to find an internship.

Ji-eun:　It's not so hard, Won-shin. Do you have your (3) _____ (4) _____ and (5) _____ ready to send out?

Won-shin:　I have those documents, but they are not (6) _____ for soliciting an internship. What can I do?

Ji-eun:　I just made a few (7) _____ to my basic documents, and that was it.

Won-shin:　Well, if that is all I have to do, then I might be more prepared than I (8) _____.

Ji-eun:　Yea, the hard part is over. You just need to tailor the cover letter.

Won-shin:　Well, I am still not sure where to begin. Do you mind giving me a (9) _____?

Ji-eun:　Sure thing. That is the least I can do for a friend.

Won-shin:　Thanks. And when I get the internship of my (10) _____, I will have you to thank.

Conversation Ⅱ

1. Listen to the conversation between the two speakers. What information has been listed about making a great cover letter?

Ji-eun: Here we go. See here, in the first paragraph, where I would normally tell a company that I found information about a job, I write that I found information about an internship.

Won-shin: I got it. And I still use the body of the letter to explain why I am qualified.

Ji-eun: Yes, that's right. Be sure, though, to include information such as when you are available, and if you expect to be paid for your work. As you may know, many internships are unpaid.

Won-shin: Great. Should I include information about my academic program and major?

Ji-eun: If you think that any information will be helpful for the reader to get to know you and your abilities, yes, include it.

Won-shin: I'll get started right away. It's just a few simple changes.

---

2. Listen again, and fill in the missing parts of speech.

Ji-eun: (1) _____. See here, in the first paragraph, where I would normally tell a company that I found information about a job, I write that I found information about an internship.

Won-shin: I got it. And I still (2) _____ to explain why I am qualified.

Ji-eun: (3) _____. Be sure, though, to include information such as when you are available, and if you expect to be paid for your work. As you may know, many internships are unpaid.

Won-shin: Great. Should I include (4) _____ academic program and major?

Ji-eun: If you think that any (5) _____ for the reader to get to know you and your abilities, yes, include it.

Won-shin: I'll get started right away. It's just a few simple changes.

Let's Get to Business

Cover Letter for an Internship Sample I

January 12, 2011

Ms. Sylvia Range
Assistant Special Programs
Marion County Family Court Wilderness Challenge
303 Center Street
Marion, VA 24560

Dear Ms. Range:

I am a junior at Eulji University, working toward my bachelor's degree in early childhood development. I am seeking an internship for the summer of 2011. While researching opportunities in the field of social welfare, I found that your program works with juvenile delinquents. I am writing to inquire about possible internship opportunities with the Marion County Family Court Wilderness Challenge.

My personal and academic background has supplied me with many skills and an understanding of dealing with the adolescent community; for example:

- I worked as a hotline assistant for a local intervention center. I counseled teenagers about personal concerns and referred them, when necessary, to appropriate professional services for additional help.

- I have been active at my university as a resident hall assistant, which requires me to establish rapport with fifty residents and advise them on personal matters, as well as university policies. In addition, I develop social and educational programs and activities each semester for up to 200 participants.

I will be in the Marion area during my spring break, March 6 - March 10. I will call you next week to see if it would be possible to meet with you in early March to discuss your program.

Please review my enclosed resume for further consideration of an internship opportunity. I would appreciate an opportunity to further discuss my skills and qualifications with you or one of your representatives. Thank you for your attention.

Sincerely,
Won-shin Cho
Won-shin Cho

Cover Letter Template

Date

Name of recipient
Recipient's title / department
Address line 1
Address line 2
Address line 3

Name of recipient:

This is where you tell the reader which internship you are applying for and where you gained knowledge of the job opening. Tell them when you want to work as an intern.

In this section list the reasons, in a graduated and logical manner, why you are qualified for this internship. Which skills do you have? What courses have you taken? What knowledge do you possess? Are you certified in something? Highlight your best professional and academic qualities.

• Use bullet points to make special experiences clear for the reader.
• You can highlight an academic experience, if you think it is related.

This is where you tell the reader how you will follow up the cover letter and resume. If you plan to send an E-mail, or make a phone call, tell them when you will write or call them.

This is your final paragraph. It is a closing statement asking the reader to review your resume, and consider you for the internship. This is also a great place to invite the reader to call you to schedule an interview. Thank the reader for their time and attention.

Sincerely,
(Signature)

Your name

Practice Makes Perfect

Write Your Own

Complete the Text

January 12, 2011
Ms. Sylvia Range
Special Programs Assistant
Marion County Family Court Wilderness Challenge
303 Center Street
Marion, VA 24560

Dear Ms. Range:

I am a (1) _____ at Eulji University, working toward my (2) _____ degree in early childhood development. I am seeking an (3) _____ for the summer of 2011. While (4) _____ opportunities in the field of social welfare, I found that your program works with juvenile delinquents. I am writing to inquire about possible internship opportunities with the Marion County Family Court Wilderness Challenge.

My personal and academic background has supplied me with many skills and an understanding of dealing with the adolescent (5) _____; for example:

I worked as a hotline (6) _____ for a local intervention center. I (7) _____ teenagers about personal concerns and referred them, when necessary, to appropriate professional services for (8) _____ help.

I have been active at my university as a resident hall assistant, (9) _____ (10) _____ me to establish (11) _____ with fifty residents and advise them on personal matters, as well as university (12) _____. In addition, I develop (13) _____ and (14) _____ programs and activities each semester, for up to 200 (15) _____.

I will be in the Marion area during my spring break, March 6 - March 10. I will call you next week to see if it would be (16) _____ to meet with you in early March to (17) _____ your program.

Please review my enclosed resume for (18) _____ consideration of an internship opportunity. I would appreciate an opportunity to further discuss my skills and qualifications with you or one of your (19) _____. Thank you for your (20) _____.

Sincerely,
Won-shin Cho
Won-shin Cho

Expressions

At the end of a cover letter, before your name, a closing phrase is used and followed by a comma.

1. Look at the following sample taken for the sample cover letter for an internship.

Sincerely,

Won-shin Cho

2. Review the expressions used for closing a letter.

Formal
- Sincerely
- Regards
- Best regards
- From
- I look forward to hearing from you soon
- Thank you for your consideration
- Thank you
- Cordially

Informal
- Warm regards
- All my best
- Thoughtful regards
- Have a nice day
- Best wishes
- Many thanks

Casual / Intimate
- Yours truly
- Love
- Affectionately
- God bless
- Warm wishes

3. Chose two closing phrases from each of the three lists above that you prefer. Circle your favorites.

> Remember that it is best to use only formal closing phrases in cover letters. Save the informal phrases for co-workers, friends and relative, and the casual and intimate closing phrases for special people, with whom you have an established relationship.

Concepts

Answer the following questions about cover letters for internships.

1) What is different about a cover letter for an internship?

2) Why do you mention payment in this type of cover letter?

3) Should you tell them about your academic interests and major? Why or why not?

4) With whom should you use formal and informal closing phrases?

5) Where in a cover letter can you invite the reader to schedule you for an interview?

Ask and You Shall Receive

Unit 3 Ask and You Shall Receive

Concepts

- Create a letter of inquiry
- Learn the difference between hard copy and e-mail versions
- Reinforce resume and interview vocabulary

Vocabulary

- Prospective
- Post
- To land the job
- Response
- Graphical
- Output
- Attached
- Division
- Application
- Position

- Traditional
- Inquiry
- In a nutshell
- Coding
- Input
- Enclosed
- Outlines
- Transcripts
- Recipient
- Asset

Let's Get Started

1. Listen to the conversation between the two speakers. What issue is being discussed?

Tyler:	Have you gotten a job lined up yet, for after graduation?
Jae-eun:	No. I am getting really nervous about it.
Tyler:	I just sent out a letter of inquiry last week to a great company in Seoul. And guess what?
Jae-eun:	What?
Tyler:	They called me and asked for an interview! It's perfect.
Jae-eun:	Sounds like a great opportunity. Did you know they were hiring?
Tyler:	No, I wasn't sure, so I sent a letter of inquiry asking about a job and telling the human resource manager a little about myself.
Jae-eun:	I think it paid off. Now, tell me, what is this letter of inquiry you are talking about?
Tyler:	It's just that. It is a letter, a lot like a cover letter. Only a letter of inquiry asks something. Inquiry is similar to the word inquire, which means to ask.
Jae-eun:	Thanks Tyler. Congratulations on your interview. I hope you land the job.
Tyler:	Well, what about you? Let's find you a great opportunity, too.
Jae-eun:	That sounds like a plan, but first I have to write my letter of inquiry.

2. Listen again, and fill in the missing parts of speech.

Tyler: Have you gotten a job lined up yet, for after (1) _____?

Jae-eun: No. I am getting really (2) _____ about it.

Tyler: I just sent out a letter of (3) _____ last week to a great company in Seoul. And guess what?

Jae-eun: What?

Tyler: They called me and asked for an (4) _____! It's perfect.

Jae-eun: Sounds like a great (5) _____. Did you know they were hiring?

Tyler: No, I wasn't sure, so I sent a letter of inquiry asking about a job and telling the human resource (6) _____ a little about myself.

Jae-eun: I think it paid off. Now, tell me, what is this letter of inquiry you are talking about?

Tyler: It's just that. It is a letter, a lot like a cover letter. Only a letter of inquiry asks something. Inquiry is similar to the word inquire, which means to ask.

Jae-eun: Thanks Tyler. (7) _____ on your interview. I hope you (8) _____ the job.

Tyler: Well, what about you? Let's (9) _____ you a great opportunity, too.

Jae-eun: That sounds like a plan, but first I have to (10) _____ my letter of inquiry.

Conversation Ⅱ

1. Listen to the conversation between the two speakers. What information has been listed about making a great cover letter?

Jae-eun: Look at this! Now I understand the difference between a cover letter and a letter of inquiry.

Tyler: Tell me what it says, and I will tell you what I think.

Jae-eun: It says that I should, politely and formally, ask if there are any career opportunities available now or in the near future.

Tyler: That's right. Go on.

Jae-eun: It also says that it should tell the reader about me and why I am a great candidate for that company.

Tyler: Ok, they've got it. That is, in a nutshell, what a letter of inquiry is. Make sure though, that you get the correct style for an e-mail. You'll get a faster response with an e-mail these days.

2. Listen again, and fill in the missing parts of speech.

Jae-eun: (1) _____! Now I understand the difference between a cover letter and a letter of inquiry.

Tyler: Tell me what it says, and (2) _____ what I think.

Jae-eun: It says that I should, (3) _____, ask if there are any career opportunities available now or in the near future.

Tyler: That's right. (4) _____.

Jae-eun: It also says that it should tell the reader about me and why I am a great candidate for that company.

Tyler: Ok, they've got it. That is, (5) _____, what a letter of inquiry is. Make sure though, that you get the correct style for an e-mail. You'll get a faster response with an e-mail these days.

Let's Get to Business

....

Letter of Inquiry Sample I

December 12, 2009

Mr. Bo-seul Lee
Template Division MEGATEK Corporation
MEGATEK Building Samseong-Dong
Gangnam-gu, Seoul
Leeboseul@megatek.com

Dear Mr. Lee:

I learned of MEGATEK through online research using the CareerSearch database through Career Services at Eulji University where I am completing my Bachelor's degree in Engineering. From my research on your web site, I believe there would be a good fit between my skills and interests and your needs. I am interested in an engineering position upon completion of my degree in February of 2010.

As a student, I am one of six members on a software development team where we are writing a computer-aided aircraft design program. My responsibilities include designing, coding, and testing of a graphical portion of the program, which requires the use of GIARO for graphics input and output. I have a strong background in computer-aided design, software development, and engineering, and believe that these skills would benefit the designing and manufacturing aspects of Template software. Attached is my resume, which further outlines my qualifications.

My qualifications make me well suited to the projects areas in which your division of MEGATEK is expanding efforts. I would appreciate the opportunity to discuss a position with you, and will contact you in ten days to answer any questions you may have and to see if you need any additional information from me such as a company application form or transcripts. Thank you for your consideration.

Sincerely,
Jae-eun Kim
Jae-eun Kim
154 Sunae-dong
Bundang-gu, Seongnam-si
+82 (10) 2345-6789
Kim.jae.eun@kmail.com

Resume attached as MS Word document

Letter of Inquiry Template

Date

Receiver's name
Address line 1
Address line 2
Address line 3
Receiver's e-mail address

Name of recipient with an opening phrase:

This is where you tell the reader how you learned about the company. Tell them that you are a good fit, or match, for what the company needs. If you are still in university, tell them when you will finish and with which type of degree.

This is a paragraph regarding skills, knowledge and abilities. This can include personal experiences, related to professional, intern or academic experiences that will help the reader get to know you. Create a clear understanding of who you are. Sell yourself.

This is your final paragraph. It is a closing statement asking the reader to review your resume, and consider you for the job. Remind the reader that you would be an asset to the company. Tell the reader that you will follow up with another e-mail or phone call in a determined amount of time. If you tell them 10 days, you must call or write in 10 days. Thank the reader for their time and attention.

Sincerely,
Signature
Your name
Address line 1
Address line 2
Address line 3
Your e-mail address

Resume attached as MS Word document

Practice Makes Perfect

Write Your Own

Complete the Text

December 12, 2009

Mr. Lee Bo Seul
Template (1) _____ MEGATEK Corporation
MEGATEK (2) _____ Samseong-dong
Gangnam-gu, Seoul
Leeboseul@megatek.com

Dear Mr. Burns:

I learned of MEGATEK through online research using the CareerSearch (3) _____ through (4) _____ (5) _____ at Eulji University where I am (6) _____ my Bachelor's degree in Engineering. From my research on your web site, I believe there would be a good fit between my skills and interests and your needs. I am interested in an engineering position (7) _____ (8) _____ of my degree in February of 2010.

As a student, I am one of six members on a software development team where we are writing a computer-aided aircraft design program. My (9) _____ include designing, coding, and testing of a graphical portion of the program, which requires the use of GIARO for graphics input and output. I have a (10) _____ (11) _____ in computer-aided design, software development, and engineering, and believe that these skills would benefit the designing and (12) _____ aspects of Template software. Attached is my resume, which further outlines my qualifications.

My (13) _____ make me (14) _____ (15) _____ to the projects areas in which your division of MEGATEK is expanding efforts. I would appreciate the opportunity to discuss a (16) _____ with you, and will (17) _____ you in ten days to answer any questions you may have and to see if you need any (18) _____ information from me such as a company application form or (19) _____. Thank you for your (20) _____.

Sincerely,
Jae-Eun Kim
Jae-Eun Kim
154 Sunae-dong
Bundang-gu, Seongnam-si
+82 (10) 2345-6789
Kim.jae.eun@kmail.com

Resume attached as MS Word document

Hard Copy versus E-Mail

Cover letters, business letters and letters of inquiry, along with a resume, can be sent either by traditional post, or e-mail. Nowadays, it is becoming very popular to advertise for jobs via the Internet and e-mail.
Read the following guidelines for sending letters and resumes.

Traditional Post: When you send a cover letter or resume to a prospective employer, it is important to provide the whole address, to ensure that the package arrives. If you are sending the package overseas, be sure to mark the destination country in all capital letters. Be sure that you have also included your own address, in full, for the return mail. Also, the name of the receiver should come first when you send a letter in hard copy. Followed, then, by the address and date. Last, you begin the body of your letter with an opening statement. If you have sent additional materials with the letter, they are listed as "enclosures" at the very end of your letter. (See Cover Letter Sample 1)

E-Mail: E-mailed letters are similar, but a few changes should be made. Start an e-mail with the date. Follow that with the name and address of the receiver. Then, being the letter with an opening statement. Make sure that the actual e-mail address that you use sounds professional. If you were 15 years old and thought that a great e-mail address would be poopisgreat@kmail.com, it might be time for a change. Do your best to look professional from every angle. Also, at the end of the letter, if you have attached and documents, such as your resume, to the e-mail, list them as "attached as a _____ document." In the blank, list the program with which you created the document. If you used Hansoft, Microsoft Word, etc., list it there. Remember, that English is best written in computer software meant for the English Language.

****It is likely that non-Korean people will NOT have Hansoft installed on their computers. That means they will never read your resume. Be sure to think of all the details before you hit "send."****

Concepts

Answer the following questions about letters of inquiry.

1) What is the main idea of a letter of inquiry?

2) What information is included in the first paragraph?

3) What information is included in the second paragraph?

4) What is the primary difference between a cover letter and a letter of inquiry?

5) What should you do if you say you will call or write in 10 days?

Back to Basics

Unit 4   Back to Basics

 Concepts

- Create a basic resume
- Learn about the personal information section of your resume
- Reinforce resume and interview vocabulary

Vocabulary

- Objective
- Profession
- Terminology
- Mature
- Mentor
- Basis
- Operated
- To support
- Machinery

- Medical
- Exceptional
- Diligent
- Concerns
- Duties
- Requirements
- Performed
- Frequently
- Associates

Let's Get Started

1. Listen to the conversation between the two speakers. What issue is being discussed?

Min-young: Hey, Jamie. Did you hear about the resume writing class that is being offered at the Career Center?

Jamie: Yes, sure. I was just going to sign up for it. I heard the participants come out with really great resumes.

Min-young: And a great resume gets you the interview you need to get a job.

Jamie: Right. And I really want a good job when I graduate.

Min-young: Then we should hurry and get our names on the list before the class fills up. A great resume isn't easy to write if you don't know where to begin.

Jamie: I agree. There is nothing worse than missing out on an opportunity like this.

Min-young: Well said. So, when we are in class, let's help each other out.

Jamie: What do you mean?

Min-young: I'll edit yours, if you edit mine. Deal?

Jamie: Sure. It's a deal.

Min-young: Here goes nothing!

Jamie: It's all on the line now.

---

2. Listen again, and fill in the missing parts of speech.

Min-young: Hey, Jamie. Did you hear about the resume writing class that is being (1) _____ at the Career Center?

Jamie: Yes, sure. I was just going to sign up for it. I heard the (2) _____ come out with really great resumes.

Min-young: And a great resume gets you the (3) _____ you need to get a job.

Jamie: Right. And I really want a good job when I graduate.

Min-young: Then we should hurry and get our names on the list before the class fills up. A great resume isn't easy to write if you don't know where to begin.

Jamie: I agree. There is nothing worse than (4) _____ out on an opportunity like this.

Min-young: Well said. So, when we are in class, let's help (5) _____ other out.

Jamie: What do you mean?

Min-young: I'll (6) _____ yours, if you edit (7) _____. (8) _____?

Jamie: (9) _____. It's a deal.

Min-young: Here goes (10) _____!

Jamie: It's all on the line now.

Conversation Ⅱ

1. Listen to the conversation between the two speakers. What information has been listed about making a great resume?

Jae-eun: So, let's review what we have learned about a basic resume.

Min-young: First, there is the personal information section, then the objective, skills, education, and experience sections follow.

Jae-eun: We learned that it is also a good idea to include a header and footer with an e-mail address and telephone number. It looks more professional.

Min-young: That's right. Go on.

Jae-eun: Well, there is a special style of writing used for resumes.

Min-young: Let's take one step at a time. How about we look at the template again?

2. Listen again, and fill in the missing parts of speech.

Jae-eun: So, (1) _____ what we have learned about a basic resume.

Min-young: First, there is (2) _____, then the objective, skills, education, and experience sections follow.

Jae-eun: We learned that (3) _____ to include a header and footer with an e-mail address and telephone number. It looks more professional.

Min-young: That's right. Go on.

Jae-eun: Well, there is (4) _____ used for resumes.

Min-young: Let's take (5) _____. How about we look at the template again?

Let's Get to Business

Basic Resume Sample I

DR. SCOTT ARMATIS, D.C.
7540 Cantaloupe Road #N, Citrus Heights, CA 95610
(815) 223-2168 - scott@yahoo.com
Single, U.S. Resident, Native English Speaker

OBJECTIVE

To teach medical English, in South Korea, in a professional environment.

SKILLS

- Exceptional English speaking, reading and presentation skills
- Conversational and Medical English terminology
- Diligent
- Mature
- Group instruction and teaching

EDUCATION

2002-2005   Western States Chiropractic College   Portland, OR
- Doctor of Chiropractic degree
- Educated patients on health problems and concerns on a daily basis.
- Operated a school information booth, which offered public education presentations, and answered general questions on healthcare.
- Offered tutoring and mentoring to newer students on a daily basis.

2001-2002   Cleveland Chiropractic College   Kansas City, MO
- Pre-professional sciences program
- Worked at the student computer lab help desk. Job duties included assisting other students with computer problems, and assistance with course assignments.

1996-1999   Clark College   Vancouver, WA
- Computer Science/General requirements
- Dean's (honors) list

EXPERIENCE

June 2007-Present   Scott Chiropractic   Lincoln, CA
Owner/Physician
- Operated a small Chiropractic practice in Lincoln, California.
- Provided health counseling and counseling on a daily basis.
- Delivered health related public seminars on a monthly basis.

2005-2007   ZLB Plasma Services   Portland, OR
Medical Staff Associate
- Performed physical examinations and instructed new donors on laboratory procedures.
- Assisted in the training of new staff in office and equipment procedures.
- Assisted in the mentoring of new medical staff associates.

ACTIVITIES AND INTERESTS

Social Networking Service for New Technology / Society for New World New York
Co-ordinator

AWARDS AND HONORS

Grand Prize for an Honorable Chiropractor
Awarded to a Distinguished Chiropractor by International Chiropractic Association

(815) 223-2168 • E-MAIL SCOTT@YAHOO.COM
7540 CANTELOPE ROAD #N • CITRUS HEIGHTS, CALIFORNIA 95610

Basic Resume 1 Template

YOUR NAME

Your address line 1
Phone number - youremail@yahoo.com
Basic personal information line

OBJECTIVE

This is where you state your objective

SKILLS

- List skills that are important for the position you are applying for
- Skill 2
- Skill 3
- Skill 4
- Skill 5

EDUCATION

Year	NAME OF SCHOOL	LOCATION

- Degree type
- Honors, GPA, etc.

Year	NAME OF SCHOOL	LOCATION

- Degree type
- Honors, GPA, etc.

Year	NAME OF SCHOOL	LOCATION

- Degree type
- Honors, GPA, etc.

EXPERIENCE

DATE	NAME OF COMPANY	LOCATION

Your position
- Your duties, listed in order of importance. Do not use the word "I" here. Instead, use verbs, conjugated in the PAST tense. Use POWERWORDS in this section.
- Duties 2
- Duties 3

DATE	NAME OF COMPANY	LOCATION

Your position
- Your duties, listed in order of importance. Do not use the word "I" here. Instead, use verbs, conjugated in the PAST tense. Use POWERWORDS in this section.
- Duties 2
- Duties 3

ACTIVITIES AND INTERESTS

Activity / club name	LOCATION

Your position

AWARDS AND HONORS

Award name
Description of award or honor received.

(999) 9999-9999 • E-MAIL YOUREMAIL@YAHOO.COM
YOUR ADDRESS, CITY, STATE, COUNTRY

Practice Makes Perfect

Write Your Own

_____

_____

_____

OBJECTIVE

This is where you state your objective

SKILLS

-
-
-

EDUCATION

-
-

-

EXPERIENCE

-
-
-

ACTIVITIES AND INTERESTS

_____

_____

AWARDS AND HONORS

_____

_____

( ) _____-_____ • E-MAIL _____@_____._____

Complete the Text

DR. SCOTT ARMATIS, D.C.

7540 Cantaloupe Road #N, Citrus Heights, CA 95610
(815) 223-2168 - scott@yahoo.com
Single, U.S. Resident, Native English Speaker

(1) _____

To teach (2) _____ English, in South Korea, in a (3) _____ environment.

SKILLS

- (4) _____ English speaking, reading and presentation skills
- Conversational and Medical English (5) _____
- (6) _____
- (7) _____
- Group instruction and teaching

EDUCATION

2002-2005   Western States Chiropractic College   Portland, OR
- Doctor of Chiropractic degree
- Educated patients on health problems and (8) _____ on a daily basis.
- Operated a school information booth, which offered public education presentations, and answered general questions on healthcare.
- Offered tutoring and (9) _____ to newer students on a daily (10) _ ___.

2001-2002   Cleveland Chiropractic College   Kansas City, MO
- Pre-professional sciences program
- Worked at the student computer lab help desk. Job (11) _____ included assisting other students with computer problems, and assistance with course assignments.

1996-1999   Clark College   Vancouver, WA
- Computer Science/General (12) _____
- Dean's (honors) list

EXPERIENCE

June 2007-Present   Scott Chiropractic   Lincoln, CA
Owner/Physician
- (13) _____ a small Chiropractic practice in Lincoln, California.
- (14) _____ health counseling and counseling on a daily basis.
- (15) _____ health related public seminars on a monthly basis.

2005-2007   ZLB Plasma Services   Portland, OR
Medical Staff Associate
- (16) _____ physical examinations and instructed new donors on laboratory procedures.
- Assisted in the training of new staff in office and equipment procedures.
- Assisted in the mentoring of new medical staff (17) _____.

ACTIVITIES AND INTERESTS

Social Networking Service for New Technology / Society for New World New York Co-ordinator

AWARDS AND HONORS

Grand Prize for an Honorable Chiropractor
Awarded to a Distinguished Chiropractor by International Chiropractic Association

(815) 223-2168 • E-MAIL SCOTT@YAHOO.COM
7540 CANTELOPE ROAD #N • CITRUS HEIGHTS, CALIFORNIA 95610

Heading and Personal Information Section

1. Read the following information about your personal information. Review the name address and telephone number sections.

> Your Name: Since your name is probably the most important piece of information on your resume, you want it to be seen quickly and easily. Place your name in the **top middle** or the **upper-right corner** of the page. Why? After your resume is read, it will probably go into a filing cabinet with the left-hand side of the paper placed against the spine of a folder. Your name will be noticed easily if it's in the top middle or in the upper-right corner of the page.

> **Address:** Putting your street address in your heading conjures up a stable image of home. If, however, you have a specific reason not to give out your street address, it's acceptable to use a post office address, or a general city or neighborhood, as a location.

> **Phone number:** List your work number on your resume only if you can talk freely from that phone and a message can be left without jeopardizing your job. Never assume that a caller will be discreet on your behalf. If you list a cell phone, be sure to answer the phone in a professional manner in times of a job search.

> **Email address:** Listing your email address in the heading section can be beneficial to your job search. Providing your email address will often expedite the employer's response, while demonstrating that you're Internet and computer savvy, a plus when applying for many positions. Be sure that it is up to date, and professionally appropriate.

Heading and Personal Information

1. Review the following example and template for a resume heading.

A	**SEONGJAE KIM / REPUBLIC OF KOREA** Gwangmyeong 2-dong Gwangmyeong-si Gyeonggi-do 82-10-3012-7256 seong_Jae@naver.com

B	**NAME / NATIONALITY** XXX-dong XXX-gu XXX-si 000-0000-0000 Youremailhere@yahoo.com

C	**CHARLOTTE MAE / US CITIZEN** 123 Del Pueblo, Yuma, Arizona 503-656-1844 charlotte.mae@yahoo.com

D	**NAME / NATIONALITY** Street address, City, State / province 000-0000-0000 • Youremailhere@yahoo.com

2. Create your own heading in the template below.

NAME / NATIONALITY

XXX-dong XXX-gu XXX-si

000-0000-0000 • Youremailhere@yahoo.com

_____ / _____

_____ - _____ - _____

_____ - _____ - _____   _____@_____

Concepts

Answer the following questions about basic resumes.

1) What is the main purpose of a resume?

2) What sections are included in a basic resume?

3) What is the most important piece of information on your resume?

4) Where should your name be located on the resume? Why?

5) What are some important rules for phone numbers listed on your resume?

Skills, Skills, Skills

Unit 5　Skills, Skills, Skills

Concepts

- Create a skill-based resume
- Learn about the summary of qualifications section of your resume
- Reinforce resume and interview vocabulary

Vocabulary

- Management
- Public relations
- Brochure
- To manage
- To assist
- Coordinated
- To distribute
- Conversational
- National
- Primary
- Trainee
- Potential
- Campaign
- To arrange
- Chronological
- Multimedia
- Billboards
- Partnership
- Marketing
- Skill-based

Let's Get Started

Conversation Ⅰ

1. Listen to the conversation between the two speakers. What issue is being discussed?

Kelly:	Well, I finally finished my first draft of my basic resume.
Jacob:	Congratulations. That is quite an accomplishment.
Kelly:	I heard, though, that there are other resume styles and formats.
Jacob:	Yes, it's true. There are many. The most popular styles include chronological, skill-based and career-focused.
Kelly:	Well, I should have one of each on file in my computer, so that, at any moment, I can recall it, and send it. It's a great strategy, don't you think?
Jacob:	Sure, that's why I just finished my skill-based resume. It really communicates my skills, knowledge and abilities well.
Kelly:	Wow, I am envious. I want one, too. Can I see yours?
Jacob:	Yea, take a look. I have it right here.

2. Listen again, and fill in the missing parts of speech.

Kelly: Well, I (1) _____ finished my first (2) _____ of my basic resume.

Jacob: Congratulations. That is quite an (3) _____.

Kelly: I heard, though, that there are other resume styles and (4) _____.

Jacob: Yes, it's true. There are many. The most (5) _____ styles include chronological, (6) _____ and career-focused.

Kelly: Well, I should have one of each on file in my computer, so that, at any (7) _____, I can recall it, and send it. It's a great (8) _____, don't you think?

Jacob: Sure, that's why I just finished my skill-based resume. It really communicates my skills, (9) _____ and abilities well.

Kelly: Wow, I am (10) _____. I want one, too. Can I see yours?

Jacob: Yea, take a look. I have it right here.

Conversation Ⅱ

1. Listen to the conversation between the two speakers. What information has been listed about making a great resume?

Kelly: So, what is the primary difference between a basic resume and a skill-based resume?

Jacob: The biggest difference is the focus of the information. A skill-based resume focuses on what you can do, rather than where you have worked.

Kelly: So, I still list my past work or professional experience?

Jacob: Of course, but you unpack more skills, in detail. It helps the reader understand exactly what you can contribute to the job.

Kelly: Do I simply make a list?

Jacob: Well, it's more complicated than that. I like to use subcategories, and bullet points to make the skills and qualifications easier to read.

Listen again, and fill in the missing parts of speech. 🔊 Audio

Kelly: So, what is the primary (1) _____ a basic resume and a skill-based resume?

Jacob: The biggest difference is the focus of the information. A skill-based resume (2) _____, rather than where you have worked.

Kelly: So, I still list my past work or professional experience?

Jacob: Of course, but you unpack more skills, in detail. It helps the reader understand exactly what (3) _____.

Kelly: Do I (4) _____?

Jacob: Well, it's more complicated than that. I like to use subcategories, and bullet points to make the skills and (5) _____ _____.

Let's Get to Business

Skill-based Resume Sample I

Jacob A. Kelly

600 Jackson St., Apt. C • Portland, OR   24060 • (503) 555-2121 • Email: jakelly@psu.edu

---

OBJECTIVE

Sales management trainee position; goal to lead and train a sales staff

---

EDUCATION

Bachelor of Art, Communication Studies, Public Relations, Marketing Minor, December 2008
Portland State University, Portland, OR
Semester at Sea, Spring 2006
GPA: In-major: 3.8./4.0   Overall: 3.6/4.0
Earned 50% of educational expenses

SKILLS

Marketing / Sales / Promotion
 Cold canvassed community for potential clients
 Created informational brochure for apartment leasing company
 Developed advertising campaign for class project

Management / Training / Organizational Ability
 Managed daily activities of own painting business including renting/purchasing equipment and
 supplies, hiring assistants, budgeting, payroll
 Arranged client contracts for painting business
 Assisted in organizing talent show and benefit auction for Semester at Sea
 Coordinated sales presentation strategy for fraternity car show and trained others in sales techniques

Communications / Language / Creative Projects
 Created multimedia presentation using slides, music, and narration to brief incoming Virginia Tech
 students during orientation
 Developed sales presentations and assisted with advertising campaigns including radio spots,
 newspaper ads, billboards, posters, brochures
 Designed and distributed flyers for painting business
 Traveled around the world with Semester at Sea and used conversational Spanish skills

---

WORK EXPERIENCE

Self-Employed, (Partnership) Sunrise Painters, Salem, OR, Summer 2006
Waiter, Leonard's of Washington, Washington, DC, Summer of 2003, 2004, 2005

ACTIVITIES

Pi Sigma Epsilon - National professional fraternity in marketing, sales management and selling
Theater Arts, Portland State University

Skill-based Resume 1 Template

YOUR NAME

STREET ADDRESS • CITY, STATE / PROVINCE ZIP CODE • (xxx) xxx-xxxx • Email: youremail@kmail.com

OBJECTIVE

List the objective or goal of the resume. Why are your sending the resume? What do you want? Also, list long term goals you may have with the company here.

EDUCATION

Degree type, Major, Date
University Name, City, State / province

SKILLS

Subcategory name
  Skill or achievement
  Skill or achievement
  Skill or achievement
  Skill or achievement

Subcategory name
  Skill or achievement
  Skill or achievement
  Skill or achievement
  Skill or achievement

Subcategory name
  Skill or achievement
  Skill or achievement
  Skill or achievement
  Skill or achievement

WORK EXPERIENCE

Position, Company name, City, State / province, Date
Position, Company name, City, State / province, Date

ACTIVITIES

Group or organization name
Description of activities and role you held in organization

Practice Makes Perfect

Write Your Own

_____

_____ • _____, _____ _____ • (__) ___-___ • Email: _____@____.__

OBJECTIVE _____
_____

EDUCATION
_____, _____, _____
_____, _____, _____

SKILLS
_____
_____
_____
_____

_____
_____
_____
_____

_____
_____
_____

WORK
EXPERIENCE
_____, _____, _____, _____, _____
_____, _____, _____, _____, _____

ACTIVITIES
_____ – _____

Complete the Text

Jacob A. Smith

600 Jackson St., Apt. C • Portland, OR   24060 • (503) 555-2121 • Email: jakesmith@psu.edu

OBJECTIVE

Sales (1) _____ (2) _____ position; goal to lead and train a sales staff

EDUCATION

Bachelor of Art, Communication Studies, (3) _____(4) _____, Marketing Minor, December 2008
Portland State University, Portland, OR

Semester at Sea, Spring 2006
GPA: Major: 3.8./4.0   Overall: 3.6/4.0
Earned 50% of educational expenses

SKILLS

Marketing / Sales / Promotion
Cold canvassed community for (5) _____ clients
Created informational (6) _____ for apartment leasing company
Developed advertising (7) _____ for class project

Management / Training / Organizational Ability
(8) _____ daily activities of own painting business including renting/purchasing equipment and supplies, hiring assistants, budgeting, payroll
(9) _____ client contracts for painting business
(10) _____ in organizing talent show and benefit auction for Semester at Sea
(11) _____ sales presentation strategy for fraternity car show and trained others in sales techniques

Communications / Language / Creative Projects
Created (12) _____ presentation using slides, music, and narration to brief incoming PSU students during orientation
Developed sales presentations and assisted with advertising campaigns including radio spots, newspaper ads, (13) _____, posters, brochures
Designed and (14) _____ flyers for painting business
Traveled around the world with Semester at Sea and used (15)_____ Spanish skills

WORK EXPERIENCE

Self-Employed, ((16) _____) Sunrise Painters, Salem, OR, (17) _____ 2006

Waiter, Leonard's of Washington, Washington, DC, Summer of 2003, 2004, 2005

(18)_____

Pi Sigma Epsilon – (19) _____ professional fraternity in (20) _____, sales management and selling

Theater Arts, Portland State University

Summary of Qualifications

Review the following example and template for a summary of qualifications.

A summary of qualifications is an easy to read, bullet point-style list of the information you know and the skills you have. In other words, it tells the reader what you can do. You can write about your experience, credentials, expertise, personal values, work ethics, background, or anything that makes you qualified for the job you're after. The summary of qualifications allows the reader to see all of your skills, abilities and knowledge on the top half of the first page.

Here are some questions and examples to help you come up with strong summary statements:

Example: Someone staying in the field of financial management might write, "I've worked as a financial manager for a mid-sized company for the last 14 years."

Summary Statement: 14 years as a financial manager of a company with current sales of $75 million.

Example: The best friend of a job hunter desiring an editorial position with a newspaper might say, "She even won the Pulitzer prize! I don't think anyone from the Examiner had ever done that before."

Summary Statement: First syndicated journalist at the Examiner to receive the Pulitzer Prize.

Example: Someone applying to be a teacher in a multilingual school might write, "I can speak Spanish, Italian, and Russian."

Summary Statement: Multilingual: Spanish/English/Italian/Russian.

JACOB A. SMITH / US CITIZEN

Sunae-dong   Bundang-gu, Seongnam-si
010-5200-7226   Jakesmith@psu.edu

• Languages: native; English, advanced; Spanish, French, basic; Korean	• Diligent
• Marketing and sales expert	• Outgoing personality
• Multimedia computer software expert	• Ability to maintain given time frames
• Multimedia presentations	• Natural leadership qualities
• Detail oriented	• Creative

NAME / NATIONALITY

XXX-dong   XXX-gu, XXX-si
000-0000-0000   Youremailhere@yahoo.com

SUMMARY OF QUALIFICATIONS

• Skill	• Skill
• Skill	• Skill
• Skill	• Skill
• Skill	• Skill
• Skill	• Skill

Create your own summary of qualifications in the template provided below. Be sure to use powerful, active words. For example, the word "created" is better than the word "made."

Powerwords

Powerwords are active and powerful verbs and adjectives that create a feeling of movement, engagement and imagery in the mind of the reader. It is very important to use powerwords in a resume. With only one or two pages of writing to convince the reader that you deserve an interview, every word counts.

1. Review the following list of powerwords.
2. Circle 10 words that describe your achievements, personality or character.

A

Accelerated	accomplished	achieved	addressed
administered	advised	allocated	answered
appeared	applied	appointed	appraised
approved	arranged	assessed	assigned
assisted	assumed	assured	audited
awarded			

B

Bought	briefed	broadened	brought
budgeted	built		

C

Cataloged	caused	changed	chaired
clarified	classified	closed	collected
combined	commented	communicated	compared
compiled	completed	computed	conceived
concluded	conducted	conceptualized	considered
consolidated	constructed	consulted	continued
contracted	controlled	converted	coordinated
corrected	counseled	counted	created
critiqued	cut		

		D	
Dealt	decided	defined	delegated
delivered	demonstrated	described	designed
determined	developed	devised	diagnosed
directed	discussed	distributed	documented
doubled			

		E	
Earned	edited	effected	eliminated
endorsed	enlarged	enlisted	ensured
entered	established	estimated	evaluated
examined	executed	expanded	expedited
experienced	experimented	explained	explored
expressed	extended		

		F	
Filed	filled	financed	focused
forecast	formulated	found	founded

		G	
Gathered	generated	graded	granted
guided			

		H	
Halved	handled	helped	

		I	
Identified	implemented	improved	incorporated
increased	indexed	initiated	influenced
innovated	inspected	installed	instituted
instructed	insured	interpreted	interviewed
introduced	invented	invested	investigated
involved	issued		

		J	
joined			

		K	
kept			

		L	
Launched	learned	leased	lectured
led	licensed	listed	logged

		M	
Made	maintained	managed	matched
measured	mediated	met	modified
monitored	motivated	moved	

		N	
Named	navigated	negotiated	

		O	
Observed	opened	operated	ordered
organized	oversaw		

		P	
Participated	perceived	performed	persuaded
planned	prepared	presented	processed
procured	programmed	prohibited	projected
promoted	proposed	provided	published
purchased			

		Q	
Qualified	questioned		

		R	
Raised	ranked	rated	realized
received	recommended	reconciled	recorded
recruited	redesigned	reduced	regulated
rehabilitated	related	reorganized	repaired
replaced	replied	reported	represented
researched	resolved	responded	restored
revamped	reviewed	revised	

		S	
Saved	scheduled	selected	served
serviced	set	set up	shaped
shared	showed	simplified	sold
solved	sorted	sought	sparked
specified	spoke	staffed	started
streamlined	strengthened	stressed	stretched
structured	studied	submitted	substituted
succeeded	suggested	summarized	superseded

supervised	surveyed	systematized	

T

Tackled	targeted	taught	terminated
tested	took	toured	traced
tracked	traded	trained	transferred
transcribed	transformed	translated	transported
traveled	treated	trimmed	tripled
turned	tutored		

U

Umpired	uncovered	understood	understudied
unified	unraveled	updated	upgraded
used	utilized		

V

Verbalized	verified	visited	

W

Waged	weighed	widened	won
worked	wrote		

Concepts

Answer the following questions about skill-based resumes.

1) What is the difference between a basic and skill-based resume?

2) What sections are included in a skill-based resume?

3) What is a subcategory referring to in the skill-based resume?

4) What are powerwords? Where do you use them?

5) What is a summary of qualifications? Why is it important?

It's All in the Timing

Unit 6 It's All in the Timing

✐ Concepts

- Create a chronological resume
- Learn about the education section of your resume
- Reinforce resume and interview vocabulary

Vocabulary

- Volunteer
- To gain
- Aggressive
- Quadrant
- Innovative
- To cooperate
- Motivated
- Description
- Approach
- Potential

- Reverse
- Task
- Successful
- Associate
- Seminar
- Superior
- Reference
- Italic
- Responsibility
- Chronological

Let's Get Started

Conversation I

1. Listen to the conversation between the two speakers. What issue is being discussed?

Daniel: I am writing a simple chronological resume today.

Yoon: Really? How is a chronological resume different from other styles?

Daniel: It focuses on time, clearly showing which jobs you had and in what order you had them.

Yoon: I see. Who is this style best for?

Daniel: A chronological resume is best for professionals with at least 5 years of work experience. If you don't have a lot of experience, it is easy to see in this resume style.

Yoon: Well, since you have a lot of experience, I think that this will work well for you.

Daniel: I think so, too. I am going to finish it, and then decide what I think.

Yoon: Be sure to show me when you are done. I am interested in the final product.

---

2. Listen again and fill in the missing parts of speech.

Daniel: I am writing a (1) _____ (2) _____ resume today.

Yoon: Really? How is a chronological resume (3) _____ from other styles?

Daniel: It (4) _____ on (5) _____, clearly showing which jobs you had and in what order you had them.

Yoon: I see. Who is this style best for?

Daniel: A chronological resume is best for (6) _____ with at least 5 years of work (7) _____. If you don't have a lot of experience, it is easy to see in this resume style.

Yoon: Well, (8) _____ you have a lot of experience, I think that this will work well for you.

Daniel: I think so, too. I am going to finish it, and then decide what I think.

Yoon: Be sure to show me when you are done. I am (9) _____ in the (10) _____ product.

Conversation Ⅱ

1. Listen to the conversation between the two speakers. What information has been listed about making a great resume?

Daniel: Have you seen my new resume?

Yoon: No, not yet. Can I see it now?

Daniel: Sure, I have it with me. See? This is the chronological resume I was telling you about.

Yoon: Yes, now I understand. The heading is at the top, like other styles, followed by the objective, professional experience in reverse chronological order, then education, extra and references. What is the extra section about?

Daniel: Since this resume focuses on experience, the extra section is where I can list additional skills, and experience.

Yoon: It looks great. Hey, you might even look better on paper than in real life!

---

2. Listen again, and fill in the missing parts of speech.

Daniel: (1) _____ my new resume?

Yoon: No, not yet. (2) _____?

Daniel: Sure, I have it with me. See? This is the chronological resume

(3) _____ about.

Yoon: Yes, now I understand. The (4) _____,

like other styles, followed by the objective, professional

experience in reverse chronological order, then education, extra

and references. What is the extra section about?

Daniel: Since this resume focuses on experience, the extra section is

where I can list additional skills, and experience.

Yoon: (5) _____. Hey, you might even look better on

paper than in real life!

Let's Get to Business

Chronological Resume Sample I

Daniel Gipson

123 Panda Circle, Clackamas, Oregon • (503) 810-3160 • dannyg@kmail.com

OBJECTIVE

To gain employment with The Velvet Hammer Coffee Company, as a sales and marketing consultant.

EXPERIENCE

Lead Marketing Manager, Yoon's Wooden Spoon, Portland, Oregon
2006-2009
Lead marketing team in aggressive and successful campaign. Increased sales by 67% in the first quarter of business. Managed 12 employees. Created creative and innovative multimedia campaigns for new brands associated with the company.

Junior Marketing Associate, Yoon's Wooden Spoon, Portland, Oregon
2005-2004
Coordinated tasks for marketing campaigns. Cooperated with superiors on campaigns. Developed ideas for research and design teams. Met all pre-established sales and marketing goals for each quarter.

EDUCATION

The University of Washington, Bachelor of Art, Mass Communication
June, 2004
Graduated with honors, GPA 3.9/4.0

EXTRA

Computer software expert, diligent team player, able to maintain given time frames. Highly motivated.

REFERENCES

Available upon request.

Chronological Resume 1 Template

Name

Mail Address, City, State, Zip Code • Phone # • Email Address

OBJECTIVE

List your goal and reason for sending the resume here.

EXPERIENCE

Job Title, Company Name, City, State
Date
Short Description

Job Title, Company Name, City, State
Date
Short Description

EDUCATION

School Name, Degree, Major
Date
Honors, Activities

EXTRA

Optional extra section for what you think is important to emphasize; for example, special skills, military experience, awards and membership in career-related professional organizations. Personal hobbies and interests are no longer included in U.S. resumes, because they have too-often given the wrong impression. If this section is more important than another, move it up in your resume. Delete this section from the resume template if you don't use it.

REFERENCES

References available on request. This resume template section is often omitted in modern resume formats, because employers now assume that applicants will provide references when asked. If you need the space, delete this section.

Practice Makes Perfect

Write Your Own

_____

_____

_____, _____, _____, _____ • __-_____ • _____

OBJECTIVE _____

_____

EXPERIENCE _____

_____, _____, _____, _____,

_____

_____

_____

_____

_____, _____, _____, _____,

_____

_____

_____

_____

EDUCATION _____

_____, _____, _____, _____,

_____

_____

EXTRA _____

_____

REFERENCES _____

_____

Complete the Text

Daniel Gipson

123 Panda Circle, Clackamas, Oregon • (503) 810-3160 • dannyg@kmail.com

OBJECTIVE

To (1)_____ (2) _____ with The Velvet Hammer Coffee Company, as a sales and marketing (3) _____.

EXPERIENCE

Lead Marketing Manager, Yoon's Wooden Spoon, Portland, Oregon
2006-2009
(4) _____ marketing team in (5) _____ and (6) _____ campaign.
(7) _____ sales by 67% in the first quarter of business. Managed 12 employees. Created (8) _____ and (9) _____ multimedia campaigns for new brands (10) _____ with the company.

Junior Marketing Associate, Yoon's Wooden Spoon, Portland, Oregon
2005-2004
Coordinated (11) _____ for marketing campaigns. (12) _____ with
(13) _____ on campaigns. Developed ideas for research and design teams.
Met all pre-(14) _____ sales and marketing (15) _____ for each quarter.

EDUCATION

The University of Washington, Bachelor of Art, Mass Communication June, 2004

Graduated with honors, GPA 3.9/4.0

EXTRA

Computer (16) _____ (17) _____, diligent (18) _____ (19) _____, able to maintain given time frames. Highly (20)_____.

REFERENCES

Available upon request.

Education

Review the following example and template for the education section of a resume.

> The education section clearly shows the reader which degree you have completed, and which is in progress. It also shows your major, minor if you had one, and any additional training, or informal certifications you may have. If you have not received your degree yet, list the word *Candidate* in place of the date.
>
> - The school name should be in **BOLD, CAPITAL LETTERS**.
> - The city and state should also be in **bold letters**.
> - The month and year the degree was awarded should be in italic letters.

JACOB A. SMITH / US CITIZEN

Sunae-dong Bundang-gu, Seongnam-si
010-5200-7226 Jakesmith@psu.edu

• Languages: native; English, advanced; Spanish, French, basic; Korean	• Diligent
• Marketing and sales expert	• Outgoing personality
• Multimedia computer software expert	• Ability to maintain given timeframes
• Multimedia presentations	• Natural leadership qualities
• Detail oriented	• Creative

EDUCATION

PORTLAND STATE UNIVERSITY, Portland, Oregon,   *June 1998*

Bachelor of Science, Biomedical Engineering

Minor in Chemistry

NAME / NATIONALITY

XXX-dong XXX-gu, XXX-si
000-0000-0000 Youremailhere@yahoo.com

SUMMARY OF QUALIFICATIONS

• Skill	• Skill
• Skill	• Skill
• Skill	• Skill

EDUCATION

SCHOOL NAME, City, State or province   *Month 19XX*

Degree type, Major

Minor

Certification

2. Create your own education section in the template provided below. Be sure to use capital letters, and italics where necessary. Follow the sample, if you need help.

NAME / NATIONALITY

XXX-dong XXX-gu, XXX-si
000-0000-0000 Youremailhere@yahoo.com

SUMMARY OF QUALIFICATIONS

• Skill	• Skill
• Skill	• Skill
• Skill	• Skill
• Skill	• Skill
• Skill	• Skill

EDUCATION

_____, _____, _____   _____ _____

_____, _____

The SEEK Approach

The SEEK Approach is a unique way of looking at yourself and your resume. SEEK stands for:

S- Skills
E- Education
E- Employment
K- Knowledge

The SEEK Approach begins with four quadrants, divided into the four categories listed above. To use this method, you must think about yourself, what you can do, what you know, and what learning experiences you have had. This method allows you to clearly see where you are weak, and where you are strong. The quadrants that list fewest achievements show where you are weak. Those that list a lot of achievements show where you are strong. The weak areas may be perceived by potential employers as reasons not to hire you. If you have a weak quadrant, it's your responsibility to strengthen that area.

1. Review the SEEK Approach template below.

SKILLS	EDUCATION
This is where you list the things you can do.	This is where you list formal, non-formal and informal education, classes, camps and seminars.

EMPLOYMENT	KNOWLEDGE
This is where you list all work experience, paid and unpaid. Any volunteer activities also go here.	What you know is different from what you can do. List your knowledge base here.

2. Complete the SEEK Approach chart below for yourself.

SKILLS	EDUCATION
EMPLOYMENT	**KNOWLEDGE**

3. Review the contents of each quadrant.
   Where are you strongest? Where are you weakest?

4. Create a goal in the space below to strengthen each area. How will you achieve your goal? Create a plan to follow through and achieve your goal.

SKILLS QUADRANT: _____

GOAL: _____

ACTION PLAN: _____

EDUCATION QUADRANT: _____

GOAL: _____

ACTION PLAN: _____

EXPERIENCE QUADRANT: _____

GOAL: _____

ACTION PLAN: _____

KNOWLEDGE QUADRANT: _____

GOAL: _____

ACTION PLAN: _____

Concepts

Answer the following questions about basic resumes.

1) What is the difference between a skill-based resume and a chronological resume?

2) What information is in the extra section?

3) Are hobbies and personal interests included in US resumes?   Why or why not?

4) What is the SEEK Approach?

5) If you have not received your degree yet, which word do you use in place of the date?

7
UNIT

Beyond Basic

You're Hired!

Unit 7　Beyond Basic

Vocabulary

- Therapy
- Emphasizing
- To diagnose
- Appropriate
- Extensive
- Analyses
- Rehabilitation
- Manual
- Project
- Significance
- Facility
- Accurately
- To determine
- To evaluate
- Functional
- Outpatient
- In-house
- Publication
- Academic
- Achievement

Let's Get Started

Conversation Ⅰ

1. Listen to the conversation between the two speakers. What issue is being discussed?

Hye-jin:	I feel like I have learned so many resume styles, but how do I know which one to choose?
David:	That's no easy task. Which one do you think suits you best?
Hye-jin:	What do you mean?
David:	What you should do is make one sample of each resume, and see which style presents you in the best possible way. Then, you can really decide which one is best for you.
Hye-jin:	Well, I think because I only graduated a couple of years ago, I might not use the chronological style, but I will try anyway. It's worth the effort to have the perfect job-winning resume.
David:	Hey, don't you mean interview-winning resume?
Hye-jin:	Well, that's what I meant. After all, the only goal of a resume is to win the interview.
David:	You catch on quickly.

2. Listen again, and fill in the missing parts of speech.

Hye-jin: I feel like I have learned so many resume (1) _____, but how do I know which one to (2) _____?

David: That's no easy (3) _____. Which one do you think (4) _____ you best?

Hye-jin: What do you mean?

David: What you should do is make one (5) _____ of each resume, and see which style presents you in the best possible way. Then, you can really (6) _____ which one is best for you.

Hye-jin: Well, I think because I only (7) _____ a couple of years ago, I might not use the chronological style, but I will try anyway. It's worth the effort to have the perfect (8) _____ _____ resume.

David: Hey, don't you mean interview-winning resume?

Hye-jin: Well, that's what I (9) _____. After all, the only goal of a resume is to win the interview.

David: You (10) _____ on quickly.

Conversation Ⅱ

1. Listen to the conversation between the two speakers. What information has been listed about making a great resume?

Hye-jin: So, what about putting one element of all of these resume styles together and creating something new?

David: Sure. Give it your best shot. What sections will you include?

Hye-jin: This modified basic resume should have a heading, objective, abilities and knowledge section, professional experience, education and a certification section.

David: What is the certification section?

Hye-jin: Since I graduated I have gained membership to several professional organizations in my field. I should put them on my resume. It shows commitment to continuing education and dedication to my profession.

David: I think this is going to be a great resume! Do you want to make one for me, too?

Hye-jin: So, (1) _____ one element of all of these resume styles together and creating something new?

David: Sure. (2) _____. What sections will you include?

Hye-jin: (3) _____ should have a heading, objective, abilities and knowledge section, professional experience, education and a certification section.

David: What is the certification section?

Hye-jin: Since I graduated I have gained membership to several professional organizations in my field. (4) _____. It shows commitment to continuing education and dedication to my profession.

David: I think this is going to be a great resume! (5) _____ _____ for me, too?

Let's Get to Business

Park Hye Jin

201 S. Second St.
Springfield, MA 01082
(719) 555 - 2736

OBJECTIVE

A position in a physical therapy facility emphasizing sports medicine, which will allow me to continue to develop my skills in manual therapy.

ABILITIES

- Accurately diagnose sprains, strains, and ruptures.
- Determine appropriate treatment for injury.
- Evaluate physical recommendations
- Motivate elderly or recently immobilized patients.
- Accurately document patient treatment and progress.
- Perform extensive patient evaluations such as range of motion and functional analyses

PROFESSIONAL EXPERIENCE

Results Fitness & Therapy, Springfield, MA
Physical Therapist, 2008 - Present
Handled care of all outpatient services. Provided physical therapy for athletes. Managed three physical therapy interns. Conducted in-house training for EMT services certificate program.

John. L. Shook Home, Boston, MA
Physical Therapist, August 2006 - 2008
Supervised 30+ elderly residents in personal physical therapy sessions. Designed exercise and rehabilitation programs.

EDUCATION

Boston University, Boston, MA
Bachelor of Science, Physical Therapy, 2006

PROFESSIONAL AFFILIATIONS AND CERTIFICATIONS

- American Association of Physical Therapists
- CPR Certification - American Heart Association
- First Aid Certification, American Red Cross

Your Name

Street Address
City, State/ Province zip code
(000) 000 - 0000

OBJECTIVE

List your goal for sending your resume. Which job do you want? Do you have any long-term goals with the company? List them here if you have any. Keep this section short, and direct. In some cases, you may want to leave this section out.

ABILITIES

- Ability / Skill / Knowledge
- Ability / Skill / Knowledge
- Ability / Skill / Knowledge
- Ability / Skill / Knowledge
- Ability / Skill / Knowledge
- Ability / Skill / Knowledge

PROFESSIONAL EXPERIENCE

Company name, City, State
Job Title, date - date
Write a short, powerful, active job description here. Use powerwords, and be sure to include information such as projects, achievements, and promotions.

Company name, City, State
Job Title, date - date
Write a short, powerful, active job description here. Use powerwords, and be sure to include information such as projects, achievements, and promotions.

EDUCATION

School Name, City, State
Degree name, Major, Date

PROFESSIONAL AFFILIATIONS AND CERTIFICATIONS

- Certification / Affiliation
- Certification / Affiliation
- Certification / Affiliation

Practice Makes Perfect

Write Your Own

<pre>
                        _____
                _____ _____ _____
        _____ , _____ _____
              (___) ____ - _____
</pre>

OBJECTIVE

_____

ABILITIES

- _____
- _____
- _____
- _____
- _____
- _____

PROFESSIONAL EXPERIENCE

_____ , _____ , _____
_____ , _____ - _____
_____
_____
_____

_____ , _____ , _____
_____ , _____ - _____
_____
_____
_____

EDUCATION

_____ , _____ , _____
_____ , _____ , _____

PROFESSIONAL AFFILIATIONS AND CERTIFICATIONS

- _____
- _____
- _____

Complete the Text

Park Hye Jin

201 S. Second St.
Springfield, MA 01082
(719) 555 - 2736

OBJECTIVE

A (1) _____ in a physical (2) _____ (3) _____ (4) _____ sports medicine, which will allow me to continue to develop my skills in manual therapy.

ABILITIES

- (5) _____ (6) _____ sprains, strains, and ruptures.
- (7) _____ (8) _____ treatment for injury.
- (9) _____ physical recommendations
- Motivate elderly or recently (10) _____ patients.
- (11) _____ document patient treatment and progress.
- Perform (12) _____ patient evaluations such as range of motion and (13) _____
- (14) _____

PROFESSIONAL EXPERIENCE

Results Fitness & Therapy, Springfield, MA
Physical Therapist, 2008 - Present
Handled care of all (15) _____ services. Provided physical therapy for (16) _____ _____. Managed three physical therapy interns. (17) _____ (18) _____ training for EMT services certificate program.

John. L. Shook Home, Boston, MA
Physical Therapist, August 2006 - 2008
Supervised 30+ elderly residents in personal physical therapy sessions. Designed exercise and (19) _____ programs.

EDUCATION

Boston University, Boston, MA
Bachelor of Science, Physical Therapy, 2006

PROFESSIONAL AFFILIATIONS AND CERTIFICATIONS

- American (20) _____ of Physical Therapists
- CPR Certification - American Heart Association
- First Aid Certification, American Red Cross

Projects and Publications

1. Review the following example and template for the projects and publications section of a resume.

> - The projects and publications section of your resume is where you can highlight participation in group academic or company projects, as well as individual activities. This is a great place to list university semester projects, senior projects and projects within your major. If you are already working, this is a perfect place to list projects in which you have participated within your company.
> - Publications, if you have had any, also go here. If you write for the university newspaper, list it here. Also, academic papers of significance to the job that you are applying for can be listed here.

KATE GARCIA / US CITIZEN

Sunae-dong Bundang-gu, Seongnam-si
010-5000-7226   K.Garcia@gmail.com

• Languages: native; English, advanced; Spanish, French, basic; Korean -	• Diligent
• Quantitative and qualitative data analysis	• Outgoing personality
• Traditional security expert	• Ability to maintain given time frames
• International development strategist	• Natural leadership qualities
• Detail oriented	• Creative

EDUCATION

PORTLAND STATE UNIVERSITY, Portland, OR   *December 2005*
Bachelor of Arts, Major in Spanish
Minor in International Studies, Latin America

PUBLICATIONS / PROJECTS

Security and Development: Haiti as a Case Study
Guyana Education Access Project: A comprehensive Program Evaluation
Colombia: Security and Development on the Border
Plan Colombia: Evaluating Efficacy in the Security and Development Sector

NAME / NATIONALITY

XXX-dong XXX-gu, XXX-si
000-0000-0000 Youremailhere@yahoo.com

SUMMARY OF QUALIFICATIONS

• Skill	• Skill
• Skill	• Skill
• Skill	• Skill
• Skill	• Skill
• Skill	• Skill

EDUCATION

SCHOOL NAME, City, State or province   *Month 20XX*
Degree type, Major
Minor
Certification

PUBLICATIONS / PROJECTS

- Project / Publication
- Project / Publication
- Project / Publication
- Project / Publication

2. Create your own education section in the template provided below. Be sure to use capital letters, and italics where necessary. Follow the sample, if you need help.

NAME / NATIONALITY

XXX-dong   XXX-gu, XXX-si
000-0000-0000   Youremailhere@yahoo.com

SUMMARY OF QUALIFICATIONS

• Skill	• Skill
• Skill	• Skill
• Skill	• Skill
• Skill	• Skill
• Skill	• Skill

EDUCATION

SCHOOL NAME, City, State or providence   *Month 20XX*

Degree type, Major
Minor
Certification

PUBLICATIONS / PROJECTS

- _____
- _____
- _____
- _____

Concepts

Answer the following questions about modified basic resumes.

1) What is the primary goal of a resume?

2) What information is included in the projects and publications section?

3) Would you include a term paper in the publications section?

4) Is it possible to modify resume styles and combine more than one template?

5) Which resume style is best for you? How will you know?

In the Meantime

Unit 8   In the Meantime

✏ Concepts

- Create a pre-professional resume
- Learn about the professional experience section of your resume
- Learn about the 3 Rs of resume writing
- Reinforce resume and interview vocabulary

Vocabulary

- Cooperative
- Fast-paced
- Committee
- Award
- Honorable
- To enrich
- To drop
- Superior
- Previous
- Collegiate

- To relate
- Council
- Distinguished
- Merit
- Professional
- Portfolio
- Specific
- Active
- Current
- Fairness

Let's Get Started

Conversation Ⅰ

1. Listen to the conversation between the two speakers. What issue is being discussed?

Seung-chul: Katie, do you know which resume style I should use since I am still a student?

Katie: Really, you can use any style you like, but I think I know one you should try.

Seung-chul: Really? Even though I am still in university?

Katie: That's the idea. You have not finished school yet, and there are places in the resume format to list that.

Seung-chul: I still have two more years of university though. Can I include achievements from high school?

Katie: Maybe. Let's look it up, and see what we can find.

Seung-chul: That sounds great. I was getting nervous about putting together a resume.

Katie: There is no sense in worrying. Do you have time now? I can help you figure this out. I remember what it was like to be in your position.

---

2. Listen again, and fill in the missing parts of speech.

Seung-chul: Katie, do you know which resume style I should use (1) _____ _____ I am still a student?

Katie: Really, you can use any style you like, but I think I know one you should (2) _____.

Seung-chul: Really? Even though I am still in (3) _____?

Katie: That's the (4) _____. You have not finished school (5) _____, and there are places in the resume (6) _____ to list that.

Seung-chul: I still have two more years of university though. Can I include (7) _____ from high school?

Katie: Maybe. Let's look it up, and see what we can find.

Seung-chul: That sounds great. I was getting (8) _____ about putting together a resume.

Katie: There is no (9) _____ in worrying. Do you have time now? I can help you figure this out. I remember what it was like to be in your (10) _____.

Conversation II

1. Listen to the conversation between the two speakers. What information has been listed about making a great resume?

Seung-chul: Here we go! This information says that on a pre-professional resume I can include high school activities until I am in my third year of university.

Katie: Well, in all fairness, by year three you should have enough collegiate activities to fill up that space.

Seung-chul: It also says that I can list activities I participate in, here at the university.

Katie: Sure. I think since you are still a student, it's important to show how involved you are at school.

Seung-chul: This is really great information. There are so many styles of resumes, it can get confusing, but I think I have found one that will work for me, at least until I graduate.

Katie: You bring up a good point. As you change, and get older, your resume style has to change, too. It's all about the 3 Rs.

Seung-chul: What are the 3 Rs?

Katie: If you have time, we will get to it later.

2. Listen again, and fill in the missing parts of speech.

Seung-chul: (1) _____! This information says that on a pre-professional resume I can include high school activities until I am in my third year of university.

Katie: Well, (2) _____, by year three you should have enough collegiate activities to fill up that space.

Seung-chul: It also says that I can list activities I participate in, here at the university.

Katie: Sure. I think since you are still a student, (3) _____ _____ how involved you are at school.

Seung-chul: This is really great information. There are so many styles of resumes, (4) _____, but I think I have found one that will work for me, at least until I graduate.

Katie: (5) _____. As you change, and get older, your resume style has to change, too. It's all about the 3 Rs.

Seung-chul: What are the 3 Rs?

Katie: If you have time, we will get to it later.

Let's Get to Business

Pre-Professional Resume Sample

SEUNG-CHUL SEONG

Gangnam-gu, Seoul, South Korea
Phone: 011-816-9773   Email: Seongsungchul@ymail.com

OBJECTIVE

Cooperative Education position related to mechanical engineering.

EDUCATION

Bachelor of Science, Mechanical Engineering, *Candidate, February 2012*
GPA: 4.0/4.5

COMPUTER SKILLS

Software:		Languages:	
AutoCAD	MiniTab	Fortran	PowerC
TK solver	Mathematica	Visual Basic	C++

EXPERIENCE

Barista, Starbucks, Seoul, Korea 2008 – present
Work 20 hours per week to help fund college education.

Server, Muscas Restaurant, Seoul, Korea, 2007 – 2008
Trained on and used excellent customer service practices in fast-paced, work environment.
Worked 35 hours per week during summer and winter vacation; worked 15 hours per week during school year.

ACTIVITIES

Student Engineers Council (SEC), Membership Committee Chair
University Symphonic Band, 2008-present
Big Brother, Big Sister Program, 2006-2009
High School Varsity Volleyball Team, 2004-2005
High School Symphonic Band, 2001-2005

HONORS

High School Distinguished Scholar, 2005
Scholar Athlete Award, 2005
Merit Award, Honorable Mention, 2005 Media Festival, Photography Division

Pre-Professional Resume Template

YOUR NAME

Address, City, State, Country
Phone: xxx-xxxx-xxxx   Email: youremailhere@ymail.com

OBJECTIVE

List goal of sending resume here. If it is a temporary or seasonal position, state that here.

EDUCATION

Bachelor of Science / Art, Major, *Candidate, Month Year*
GPA: X.X/X.X

COMPUTER SKILLS

Software:

List computer programs here.

Languages:

List computer languages here. *If you have no computer skills, change this section title. You can use language, medical machinery, etc.*

EXPERIENCE

(This is where you can list a part time job, if you have had one.)

Position, Company name, Location, Date - Date
Simple description of duties and responsibilities
List any achievements while on the job

Position, Company name, Location, Date - Date
Simple description of duties and responsibilities
List any achievements while on the job

ACTIVITIES

Program / Activity Name, Your Position, Date - Date
Program / Activity Name, Your Position, Date - Date
Program / Activity Name, Your Position, Date - Date
Program / Activity Name, Your Position, Date - Date
Program / Activity Name, Your Position, Date - Date

HONORS

Honor or Award, Date
Honor or Award, Date
Honor or Award, Date

Practice Makes Perfect

Write Your Own

_____

Phone: ____-____-____   Email: _____@_____

OBJECTIVE _____

EDUCATION _____

GPA: _____/_____

COMPUTER
SKILLS

Software: **Languages:**

_____   _____
_____   _____
_____   _____

EXPERIENCE _____

_____, _____, _____, _____ - _____
_____
_____

_____, _____, _____, _____ - _____
_____
_____

ACTIVITIES _____

_____
_____
_____

HONORS _____

_____
_____
_____

Complete the Text

SEONG SEUNG CHUL

Gangnam-gu, Seoul, South Korea
Phone: 011-816-9773   Email: Seongsungchul@ymail.com

(1) _____

(2) _____ Education position (3) _____ to mechanical engineering.

EDUCATION

Bachelor of Science, Mechanical Engineering, *(4) _____, February 2012*
GPA: 4.0/4.5

(5) _____
SKILLS

Software:		**Languages:**	
AutoCAD	MiniTab	Fortran	PowerC
TK solver	Mathematica	Visual Basic	C++

(6) _____

Barista, Starbucks, Seoul, Korea 2008 – present
Work 20 (7) _____ (8) _____ (9) _____ to help (10) _____ college education.

Server, Muscas Restaurant, Seoul, Korea, 2007 – 2008
Trained on and used excellent customer service practices in (11) _____, work environment.
Worked 35 hours per week during summer and winter vacation; worked 15 hours per week during school year.

(12) _____

Student Engineers (13) _____ (SEC), Membership (14) _____ Chair
University Symphonic Band, 2008-present
Big Brother, Big Sister Program, 2006-2009
High School Varsity Volleyball Team, 2004-2005
High School Symphonic Band, 2001-2005

(15) _____

High School (16) _____ (17) _____, 2005
Scholar Athlete (18) _____, 2005
(19) _____ Award, (20) _____ Mention, 2005 Media Festival, Photography Division.

Professional Experience

1. Review the following example and template for the professional experience section of a resume.

- The professional experience section is where you write about achievements, duties and responsibilities you had at your current and previous employers.

- Jobs, volunteer activities, church activities, internships and part time jobs can be included. Professional experience is something you have done to enrich your career portfolio. Think hard! Every experience counts.

Writing a job description requires a specific style of writing. Even if you are writing about your current job, use the **past tense. Drop the subject** from the sentence and don't forget **powerwords**.

Choose **active** and **interesting** words for the professional experience section of your resume.

Use this: Developed
Not that: Made
Use this: Participated in _____
            Attended _____
Not that: Went to ____
Use this: Great, superior
Not that: Good

KATE GARCIA / US CITIZEN

Sunae-dong Bundang-gu, Scongnam-si
010-5000-7226   K.Garcia@gmail.com

• Languages: native; English, advanced; Spanish, French, basic; Korean	• Diligent
• Quantitative and qualitative data analysis	• Outgoing personality
• Traditional security expert	• Ability to maintain given time frames
• International development strategist	• Natural leadership qualities
• Detail oriented	• Creative

EDUCATION

PORTLAND STATE UNIVERSITY, Portland, OR   *December 2005*

Bachelor of Arts, Major in Spanish
Minor in International Studies, Latin America

PUBLICATIONS / PROJECTS

- Security and Development: Haiti as a Case Study
- Guyana Education Access Project: A Comprehensive Program Evaluation
- Colombia: Security and Development on the Border
- Plan Colombia: Evaluating Efficacy in the Security and Development Sector

PROFESSIONAL EXPERIENCE

INTERNATIONAL AFFAIRS

FUNDACION NUEVA ERA / NEW ERA GALAPAGOS FOUNDATION   *2008*
Program Manager, Galpagos Islands, Ecuador, South America
Monitored and evaluated existing projects and corresponding activities.
Successfully negotiated long-term funding with provincial government.
Coordinated all international volunteer and intern activities.

SPONSORS ORGANIZED TO ASSIST REFUGEES (SOAR)   *2007*
Volunteer, Cuban Refugee Program, Portland, OR
Created and implemented a project to expand community
outreach and participation. Organized SOAR activities for Cuban
and African emigrants. Coordinated successful fundraisers for SOAR

NAME / NATIONALITY

XXX-dong   XXX-gu, XXX-si
000-0000-0000   Youremailhere@yahoo.com

SUMMARY OF QUALIFICATIONS

• Skill	• Skill
• Skill	• Skill
• Skill	• Skill
• Skill	• Skill
• Skill	• Skill

EDUCATION

SCHOOL NAME, City, State or providence   *Month 20XX*

Degree type, Major
Minor
Certification

PUBLICATIONS / PROJECTS

- Project / Publication
- Project / Publication
- Project / Publication
- Project / Publication

PROFESSIONAL EXPERIENCE

CLUSTER TITLE
COMPANY NAME   *19XX-20XX*

Your title, City, Province / Country
A brief description of your duties and accomplishments in this position.
Do not use subjects here such as I. Assume the reader knows you are talking about yourself. Use powerwords here.

CLUSTER TITLE
COMPANY NAME   *19XX-20XX*

Your title, City, Province / Country
A brief description of your duties and accomplishments in this position.
Do not use subjects here such as I. Assume the reader knows you are talking about yourself. Use powerwords here.

2. Create your own education section in the template provided below. Be sure to use capital letters, and italics where necessary. Follow the sample, if you need help.

NAME / NATIONALITY
XXX-dong   XXX-gu, XXX-si
000-0000-0000   Youremailhere@yahoo.com

SUMMARY OF QUALIFICATIONS

• Skill	• Skill
• Skill	• Skill
• Skill	• Skill
• Skill	• Skill
• Skill	• Skill

EDUCATION

SCHOOL NAME, City, State or province   *Month 20XX*

Degree type, Major
Minor
Certification

PUBLICATIONS / PROJECTS

- Project / Publication
- Project / Publication
- Project / Publication
- Project / Publication

PROFESSIONAL EXPERIENCE

_____

_____   ____-____

_____, _____, _____

_____

_____

_____

_____   ____-____

_____, _____, _____

_____

_____

The 3 Rs of Resume Writing

There are three unforgettable Rs in resume writing: Revisit, review and rewrite. The 3 Rs will help you keep your resume current, relevant and growing. Review the 3 Rs below.

R evisit your resume. This means that even when you are not searching for a job and actively sending out resumes and cover letters, you should look at your resume at least every six months. Twice a year, open your computer files, and look at your documents. Resumes are not documents you can write one time and forget about. They grow with you, professionally and personally. Therefore, it is important to revisit them, with a fresh perspective, at least once every six months.

R eview your resume. When you revisit your documents, take time to read them. Read your resume and cover letter as if it is the first time you have ever seen the documents. Use a critical eye. Look for any unnoticed error, and make the necessary changes. Has your phone number changed? Have you moved? This is the perfect time to make changes, little by little, without the stress of timelines created by a job search.

R ewrite your resume. When you review your documents, you may discover that you have grown, developed or changed from the person you were when you first wrote them. This is natural, and expected. Use this opportunity to phase-out less desirable skills from your summary of qualifications, and add new achievements to your job description. Higher language abilities, new certifications at work or school, community involvement, or a finished project or paper can all be added to your resume. Learning when to phase something out of your resume is not difficult. Only list skills that you are passionate and excited about. Remember that your resume is about your future, not your past.

Concepts

Answer the following questions about modified basic resumes.

1) How often should you review your resume?

2) What resume strategy should you use if you are still a student?

3) What are the 3 Rs? Explain what each R means.

4) Should you include information from high school if you are in university?

5) How should you write a job description? How is the writing style unique?

9
UNIT

The World
at Your Fingertips

You're Hired!

Unit 9 The World at Your Fingertips

📝 Concepts

- Create a competitive international resume
- Learn about the certification section of your resume
- Reinforce resume and interview vocabulary

Vocabulary

- To acquire
- Framework
- Implementation
- Empowerment
- Professional experience
- Department of documentation
- Translator
- Legal
- Hybrid
- Independent contractor

- Training
- Intermediate
- Specialization
- Facilitation
- Successfully
- Conflict resolution
- Late-career
- Appointment
- Cluster

Let's Get Started

Conversation I

1. Listen to the conversation between the two speakers. What issue is being discussed?

Jay:	Meredith, have you seen my latest resume? It's amazing how much I have learned about style and format!
Meredith:	Really? Another resume? What is this one for?
Jay:	It's the perfect resume for sending to international companies, and abroad.
Meredith:	What is so great about it? Did you use scented paper?
Jay:	No, no, none of that. Scented paper is for love letters, not resumes. Don't be silly. An international resume is easy to read, highlights strengths, and gives the reader all of the information he or she needs in fewer than two pages.
Meredith:	Is it fair to say, then, that the international resume is a hybrid of many types of resumes? It sounds like this style would work for anyone.
Jay:	Yea, sure. It's a hybrid. And yes, it works for everyone. From students to late-career professionals, this style makes everyone shine.

2. Listen again, and fill in the missing parts of speech.

Jay: Meredith, have you seen my (1) _____ resume? It's (2) _____ how much I have learned about style and format!

Meredith: Really? (3) _____ resume? What is this one for?

Jay: It's the perfect resume for sending to international (4) _____, and (5) _____.

Meredith: What is so great about it? Did you use (6) _____ paper?

Jay: No, no, none of that. Scented paper is for love letters, not resumes. Don't be (7) _____. An international resume is easy to read, (8) _____ strengths, and gives the reader all of the information he or she needs in fewer than two pages.

Meredith: Is it fair to say, then, that the international resume is a (9) _____ of many types of resumes? It sounds like this style would work for anyone.

Jay: Yea, sure. It's a hybrid. And yes, it works for everyone. From students to late-career professionals, this style makes everyone (10) _____.

Conversation Ⅱ

1. Listen to the conversation between the two speakers. What information has been listed about making a great international resume?

Jay: I can help you make an international resume, if you would like.

Meredith: Can you? Really? Let's do it now!

Jay: Okay, first things first. You need a header and personal information section, followed by a summary of qualifications.

Meredith: Oh, I remember the summary of qualifications. We used that in a previous resume. I think that is a great way to present myself to my future employer.

Jay: It's true. And this style also utilizes a publication section, certification section and clustering of employment and professional experience.

Meredith: You are getting a little ahead of me. Do you mind showing me an example?

Jay: Sure enough, Meredith, anything for you.

2. Listen again, and fill in the missing parts of speech.

Jay: (1) _____ make an international resume, if you would like.

Meredith: Can you? Really? (2) _____!

Jay: Okay, (3) _____. You need a header and personal information section, followed by a summary of qualifications.

Meredith: Oh, I remember the summary of qualifications. We used that in a previous resume. I think that is a great way to present myself to my future employer.

Jay: It's true. And this style also utilizes a publication section, certification section and clustering of employment and professional experience.

Meredith: You are (4) _____ of me. Do you mind showing me an example?

Jay: (5) _____, Meredith, anything for you.

Let's Get to Business

International Resume Sample

KATE GARCIA / US CITIZEN
Sunae-dong Bundang-gu, Seongnam-si
010-5000-7226   K.Garcia@gmail.com

SUMMARY OF QUALIFICATIONS

- Acquired language skills: fluent Spanish, intermediate Italian
- Strong knowledge base in Central / South American Studies
- Small arms and light weapons disarmament policy and procedures
- Knowledge of humanitarian aid delivery in post-conflict / reconstructing countries
- Technical writing / policy memorandums
- Training of trainers
- Research design

- Project design, implementation and evaluation
- Results framework and value chain analysis
- Organization strategy development
- Strategic partnering / alliance building tools
- Training of trainers facilitation techniques
- Grant / proposal writing

EDUCATION

MONTEREY INSTITUTE OF INTERNATIONAL STUDIES, Monterey, CA

Masters of Arts, International Policy Studies,   *December 2008*
Specialization in Human Security and International Development
Certificate in Development Project Management   *April 2007*

PORTLAND STATE UNIVERSITY, Portland, OR

Bachelor of Arts, Major in Spanish
Minor in International Studies, Latin America

INFLUENCE INTERNATIONAL, Seoul, Korea

Certificate in Training the Trainer   *December 200*

PUBLICATIONS / PROJECTS

- Empowerment in the Classroom: Giving Learners What They Need. 2007
- *How to Empower: The POLE Method.* 2007.
- Co-author of *The 4 C's: Communication Challenges Coreans Need to Conquer.* 2006.
- *Effective Partnering Tool-kit.* 2005.
- *Strategic Planning: An Introduction Manual for Development Workers.* 2005.
- *Introduction to Successful Facilitation Manual: Becoming an Agent of Change.* 2005.
- Security and Development: Haiti as a Case Study
- Guyana Education Access Project: A Comprehensive Program Evaluation
- Colombia: Security and Development on the Border
- Plan Colombia: Evaluating Efficacy in the Security and Development Sector

PROFESSIONAL EXPERIENCE

INTERNATIONAL AFFAIRS

FUNDACION NUEVA ERA / NEW ERA GALAPAGOS FOUNDATION   *2005*
Program Manager, Galápagos Islands, Ecuador, South America
Monitored and evaluated existing projects and corresponding activities.
Successfully negotiated long-term funding with provincial government.
Coordinated all international volunteer and inter activities.

MEXICAN CONSULATE   *2003*
Intern, Department of Documentation, Portland, OR
Managed immigration database and assisted Mexican nationals with
documentation processes and problems. Assisted consulate in technology support.

EDUCATION

BEAUMONT MIDDLE SCHOOL   *2004*
At-Risk Group Counselor, Portland, OR
Facilitated sessions for at-risk girls, grade 7 and 8. Educated girls on conflict resolution,
social and sexual behaviors and decision making skills. Topics included physical and sexual
abuse, substance abuse and living by the law.

ESCUELA BILINGUE EL ALBA   *1998-1999*
Kindergarten teacher, Honduras, Central America
Created lesson plans building vocabulary, motor skills, basic math skills, writing skills, and
character development. Conducted parent / teacher
conferences to monitor children's progress.

TRANSLATION

PASSPORT TO LANGUAGES,   *2002-2003*
Translator and Interpreter Portland, OR
Worked as an independent contractor and translated medical and legal documents.
Attended medical appointments to facilitate doctor-patient communication.

International Resume Template

NAME / NATIONALITY
XXX-dong XXX-gu, XXX-si
000-0000-0000   Youremailhere@yahoo.com

SUMMARY OF QUALIFICATIONS

- Skill
- Skill
- Skill
- Skill
- Skill

- Skill
- Skill
- Skill
- Skill
- Skill

EDUCATION

SCHOOL NAME, City, State or province   *Month 20XX*

Degree type, Major
Minor
Certifications

PROFESSIONAL PROJECTS

- Project / Publication
- Project / Publication
- Project / Publication
- Project / Publication

PROFESSIONAL EXPERIENCE

CLUSTER TITLE
COMPANY NAME   *20XX-20XX*
Your title, City, Province / Country
A brief description of your duties and accomplishments in this position.
Do not use subjects here such as I. Assume the reader knows you are talking about yourself. Use powerwords here.

CLUSTER TITLE
COMPANY NAME   *20XX-20XX*
Your title, City, Province / Country
A brief description of your duties and accomplishments in this position.

CERTIFICATIONS

CERTIFING AGENCY NAME
Certification name   *20XX*

Write Your Own

_____ / _____

___-___-___   ___-___-___, ___-___
___-_____-_____ _____@_____

SUMMARY OF QUALIFICATIONS

- _____
- _____
- _____
- _____
- _____
- _____

- _____
- _____
- _____
- _____
- _____

EDUCATION

_____, _____, _____   _____
_____, _____
_____
_____

PROFESSIONAL PROJECTS
PROFESSIONAL EXPERIENCE

_____
_____   _____-_____
_____, _____, _____
_____
_____

CERTIFICATIONS

_____
_____   _____

Complete the Text

Fill in the blanks with the missing words from the sample resume. See what you can remember on your own, and then use the sample for assistance.

KATE GARCIA / US CITIZEN

Sunae-dong   Bundang-gu, Seongnam-si
010-5000-7226   K.Garcia@gmail.com

SUMMARY OF QUALIFICATIONS

- (1) _____ language skills: fluent Spanish, (2) _____ Italian
- Strong knowledge base in Central / South American Studies
- Small arms and light weapons disarmament policy and procedures
- Knowledge of humanitarian aid delivery in post-conflict / reconstructing countries
- (3) _____ of trainers
- Research design

- Project design, (4) _____ and evaluation
- Results (5) _____ and value chain analysis
- Organization strategy development
- Strategic partnering / alliance building tools
- Training of trainers facilitation techniques

EDUCATION

MONTEREY INSTITUTE OF INTERNATIONAL STUDIES, Monterey, CA
Masters of Arts, International Policy Studies,   *December 2008*
(6) _____ in Human Security and International Development
Certificate in Development Project Management   *April 2007*

PORTLAND STATE UNIVERSITY, Portland, OR
Bachelor of Arts, Major in Spanish
Minor in International Studies, Latin America

INFLUENCE INTERNATIONAL, Seoul, Korea
Certificate in Training the Trainer   *December 2009*

PUBLICATIONS / PROJECTS

- (7) _____ in the Classroom: Giving Learners What They Need. 2007
- *How to Empower: The POLE Method.* 2007.
- *Effective Partnering Tool-kit.* 2005.
- *Strategic Planning: An Introduction Manual for Development Workers.* 2005.
- *Introduction to Successful (8) _____ Manual: Becoming an Agent of Change.* 2005.
- (9) _____ (10) _____

INTERNATIONAL AFFAIRS
FUNDACION NUEVA ERA / NEW ERA GALAPAGOS FOUNDATION *2005*
Program Manager, Galpagos Islands, Ecuador, South America
Monitored and evaluated existing projects and corresponding activities.
(11) _____ negotiated long-term funding with provincial government.
Coordinated all international volunteer and intern activities.

MEXICAN CONSULATE *2003*
Intern, (12) _____ of (13) _____, Portland, OR
Managed immigration database and assisted Mexican nationals with
documentation processes and problems. Assisted consulate in technology support.

EDUCATION
BEAUMONT MIDDLE SCHOOL *2004*
At-Risk Group Counselor, Portland, OR
Facilitated sessions for at-risk girls, grade 7 and 8. Educated girls on (14) _____ (15) _____,
social and sexual behaviors and decision making skills. Topics included physical and
sexual abuse, substance abuse and living by the law.

TRANSLATION
PASSPORT TO LANGUAGES, *2002-2003*
(16) _____ and Interpreter Portland, OR
Worked as an (17) _____ (18) _____ and translated medical and
(19) _____ documents. Attended medical (20) _____ to facilitate
doctor-patient communication.

Certifications

1. Review the following example and template for the certification section of a resume.

- Certifications are licenses, or permissions that you have to do something. Some jobs require special certifications to operate machinery, or perform certain tests. Use this place in your resume to show the reader that you are truly qualified for the job.
- A driver's license is a certification, too. If you think that you will need to drive a company car, or your own, at a prospective job, list your license to drive. Each certification is an asset.

You can become certified for something in almost any field or profession. If you have no current certifications, think about taking a class, or two. Becoming certified in computer software is a great start. If you are certified in something specialized in your major or career, even better. Certifications are a type of non-formal education. They help balance out a resume and help you get taken seriously.

You don't have a certification? Write a goal certification below that you would like to have. Be sure to include your plan for achieving it

Do you want to have fun and get certified? Try a sports certification, like SCUBA, or becoming a personal trainer.

Certification: _____

Plan: _____

Achieve by this date: _____

2. Create your own certification section in the template provided below. Be sure to use capital letters, and italics where necessary. Follow the sample, if you need help.

NAME / NATIONALITY

XXX-dong   XXX-gu, XXX-si
000-0000-0000   Youremailhere@yahoo.com

SUMMARY OF QUALIFICATIONS

• Skill	• Skill
• Skill	• Skill
• Skill	• Skill
• Skill	• Skill
• Skill	• Skill

EDUCATION

SCHOOL NAME, City, State or province   *Month 20XX*

Degree type, Major
Minor
Certification

PUBLICATIONS / PROJECTS

• Project / Publication
• Project / Publication
• Project / Publication
• Project / Publication

PROFESSIONAL EXPERIENCE

CLUSTER TITLE

COMPANY NAME   *19XX-20XX*

Your title, City, Province / Country
A brief description of your duties and accomplishments in this position.
Do not use subjects here such as I. Assume the reader knows you are talking about yourself. Use powerwords here.

CERTIFICATIONS

_____   _____

_____

_____   _____

_____

Optional and Expanded Sections

For resumes written in English, but being sent to companies in Asia, the personal information section may need additional information. Asian companies often want to know more personal information than international companies. When in doubt, follow the guidelines given to you in the advertisement, or through your contacts at the company where you are applying.

The following information can be added to resumes being sent to Asian companies:

- Marital Status (single, married, widowed, divorced)
- Age / birth date
- Family member's names and ages
- Height
- Weight
- Religion (Christian, Buddhist, Muslim, Baha'i, etc.)
- Recent photograph
- Personal interests / hobbies

Review the following template

MIN-JI KIM / KOREAN CITIZEN

Samseong-dong   Gangnam-gu, Seoul
011-456-7890   kimminji@skymail.com
Marital Status: Single   Age: 34   Height: 164cm   Weight: 60 kg

Resume Length

The length of your resume is important. If it is too short, you might look under-qualified. If it is too long, the reader will be burdened and will not bother to read all of your skills and qualifications. Follow the following guidelines for resume length.

- **A resume should never be longer than two pages, and never shorter than one full page.** One full page of information is better than one full page and ¼ of the second page. The "short" second page leaves the reader believing that you don't have "enough" experience to fill the resume. In short, big, white, empty spaces on the pages of your resume are bad.

- **If you have more than two pages of information for your resume, trim away the experiences that don't reflect the skills for the job that you want.** If you were a waiter at a family restaurant last summer, but want to work in a hospital after you graduate, consider removing the previous job, if you have more current and professional experience. Remember that ALL experiences, paid, volunteer, academic, and religious are great for your resume. Sometimes unpaid work is more relevant than previous paid work.

- **If you are short and need "filler", an optional section might be right for you.** If you live in Korea, a section including personal interests and hobbies can be included at the end of your resume. This is appropriate only for resumes being sent to Asian / Korean companies. Be sure only to include personal interests that help you look interesting, active, well balanced and professional. See the template below for reference.

PERSONAL INTERESTS

- Hiking
- Reading

Concepts

Answer the following questions about modified basic resumes.

1) Who can use an international resume?

2) How is an international resume style beneficial?

3) Is it acceptable to use special paper, such as scented paper, for a resume? Why do you think so?

4) How many pages should your resume be? Why do you think so? What happens if it is too long? Too short?

5) Which strategy can you use to help your resume appear longer, if it too short?

UNIT 10

Mind Your Manners

Unit 10 Mind Your Manners

✏ **Concepts**

- Create a follow-up letter
- Learn the difference between e-mail and traditional post follow-up letters
- Reinforce resume and interview vocabulary

Vocabulary

- Follow-up
- To appreciate
- To experience
- To explore
- To arrange
- Interdisciplinary
- Faculty
- Problem-solving
- Constraint
- To pull up

- Advice
- To invite
- Hands-on
- Possibility
- To mention
- Intense
- Valuable
- Effective
- To justify (format)
- Brilliant

Let's Get Started

Conversation I

1. Listen to the conversation between the two speakers. What issue is being discussed?

Matt:	Ji-sun, my professor told me today that I should write a follow-up letter to the company that I had an interview with last week. Do you know anything about follow-up letters?
Ji-sun:	Sure thing, Matt. I just wrote mine for a meeting I had with a leisure design company in Seoul. I really want an internship with them next winter, so I want to stay in contact.
Matt:	Perhaps you can lend me a hand. I would love to take a look at your letter for a little inspiration.
Ji-sun:	Matt, you make me laugh. If you want my help, just ask.
Matt:	Okay, Ji-sun, can you please help me write a follow-up letter?
Ji-sun:	Yes, I will. See, that wasn't so hard, now, was it? Take a look at my computer screen. I pulled up the letter so you can check it out.
Matt:	This looks great. You thanked them for seeing you and giving you advice, and began to plan for the future.
Ji-sun:	That's the idea. A follow-up letter is the perfect detail after an important phone call, meeting, or exchange. It shows you are professional.
Matt:	Brilliant! I like the idea. I come across as professional and they see my name again and remember meeting me. This way it's hard for them to forget who I am.
Ji-sun:	Follow-up letters increase your chances of getting hired and making a good first impression.
Matt:	Well, how should I start? Let me take a closer look at yours. I need a few good ideas.

2. Listen again, and fill in the missing parts of speech.

Matt:	Ji-sun, my (1) _____ told me today that I should write a follow-up letter to the company that I had an interview with last week. Do you know anything about (2) _____ letters?
Ji-sun:	Sure thing, Matt. I just wrote mine for a (3) _____ I had with a leisure design company in Seoul. I really want an internship with them next winter, so I want to stay in contact.
Matt:	(4) _____ you can lend me a hand. I would love to take a look at your letter for a little inspiration.
Ji-sun:	Matt, you make me laugh. If you want my help, just ask.
Matt:	Okay, Ji-sun, can you please help me write a follow-up letter?
Ji-sun:	Yes, I will. See, that wasn't so hard, now, was it? Take a look at my computer screen. I (5) _____ the letter so you can check it out.
Matt:	This looks great. You thanked them for seeing you and giving you (6) _____, and began to plan for the future.
Ji-sun:	That's the idea. A follow-up letter is the perfect (7) _____ after an important phone call, meeting, or exchange. It shows you are professional.
Matt:	(8) _____! I like the idea. I come across as professional and they see my name again and remember meeting me. This way it's hard for them to forget who I am.
Ji-sun:	Follow-up letters (9) _____ your chances of getting hired and making a good first (10) _____.
Matt:	Well, how should I start? Let me take a closer look at yours. I need a few good ideas.

1. Listen to the conversation between the two speakers. What information has been listed about making a great cover letter?

Ji-sun: Okay, Matt, check this out! The first thing you do is begin with your own address. Don't include your name. They'll know by the signature who you are.

Matt: I see, and then I continue with my phone number and e-mail address. Next, I write the date, followed by the reader's name and address.

Ji-sun: I think you are beginning to understand. The rest of the letter is just like a standard business letter. Everything is lined up on the left and justified, so the lines of print go all the way across the page.

Matt: It looks neat and clean when it's justified.

Ji-sun: If you mail the letter, don't forget to sign it with a blue or black pen.

Matt: And if I e-mail it, I just type my signature.

Ji-sun: Okay, Matt, (1) _____! The first thing you do is begin with your own address. Don't include your name. They'll know by the signature who you are.

Matt: I see, and (2) _____ my phone number and e-mail address. Next, I write the date, followed by the reader's name and address.

Ji-sun: I think you are beginning to understand. (3) _____ is just like a standard business letter. Everything is lined up on the left and justified, so the lines of print go all the way across the page.

Matt: (4) _____ when it's justified.

Ji-sun: If you mail the letter, (5) _____ with a blue or black pen.

Matt: And if I e-mail it, I just type my signature.

Let's Get to Business

Follow-Up Letter Sample

501-3 Migeum-dong, Bundang-gu
Seongnam-si, ROK
+82 (10) 1234-5678
abcde@kmail.com

June 26, 2011

Ms. Emily Hall
30 Samseong-dong, Gangnam-gu
Seoul, ROK

Dear Ms. Hall:

Thank you so much for your time and advice during my visit to your office last week.

I very much appreciate your inviting me to visit since this was my first experience seeing the hands-on work, which takes place in a design department. I learned a great deal, and hope to share what I learned with members of our student chapter of the Korean Society of Leisure Design.

After July, I will be in contact with you again to explore the possibility of arranging a winter internship with your firm. As I mentioned to you when we met, I had an opportunity to work on an intense, four-day interdisciplinary project judged by faculty in which my team received top honors. I gained valuable teamwork, problem-solving and presentation skills and learned to work effectively with students studying to enter different professions. I believe my skills would make me an asset to an organization like yours, which often must produce excellent work under tight time constraints.

Thank you again for all your help, and I look forward to talking with you in the coming months.

Sincerely,

Ji-sun Kim

Ji-sun Kim

Follow-Up Letter Template

Your address line 1
Your address line 2
Your telephone number
Your e-mail address

Date

Receiver's name
Receiver's address line 1
Receiver's address line 2

Opening phrase:

Thank the reader for the meeting. Be sure to mention when and where the meeting took place. This will help the reader remember you.

Tell the reader why you are thankful for the meeting and what you gained from the meeting. Mention the name of your organization, if you have one, and how that organization is connected to the company or person reading this letter.

Tell the reader when you plan to contact them again. Also mention to the reader what you hope to initiate from any future meetings. Begin, in this paragraph, to lay groundwork for future plans together. If you want to work for this individual or company, mention that here. Take time to mention details such as projects, department names or personal contacts here.

Thank the reader one more time. Tell them that you plan and look forward to meeting with them in the future.

Letter closing,

(signature)

Your name

Practice Makes Perfect

Write Your Own

Complete the Text

501-3 Migeum-dong, Bundang-gu
Seongnam-si, ROK
+82 (10) 1234-5678
abcde@kmail.com

June 26, 2011

Ms. Emily Hall
30 Samseong-dong, Gangnam-gu
Seoul, ROK

Dear Ms. Hall:

Thank you so much for your time and (1) _____ during my visit to your office last week.

I very much (2) _____ your (3) _____ me to visit since this was my first (4) _____ seeing the (5) _____- (6) _____ work, which takes place in a design department. I learned a great deal, and hope to share what I learned with members of our student chapter of the Korean Society of Leisure Design.

After July, I will be in contact with you again to (7) _____ the (8) _____ of (9) _____ a winter internship with your firm. As I (10) _____ to you when we met, I had an opportunity to work on an (11) _____, four-day (12) _____ project judged by (13) _____ in which my team received top honors. I gained (14) _____ teamwork, (15) _____- (16) _____ and presentation skills and learned to work (17) _____ with students studying to enter different professions. I believe my skills would make me an asset to an organization like yours, which often must produce excellent work under tight time (18) _____.

Thank you again for all your help, and I look forward to talking with you in the (19) _____ months.

(20) _____,

(signature)

Ji-sun Kim

Working with Words

Active Adjectives

Cover letters, business letters and letters of inquiry, along with a resume, are best written with active adjectives that reflect your character, personality and work style. Try using a few of the following active adjectives in your letters.

1. Read the following adjectives.
2. Circle 5 adjectives that you can use to describe yourself.

Determined	Hard-working
Diligent	Trustworthy
Cooperative	Motivated
Reliable	Self-starting
Loyal	Studious
Attentive	Conscientious
Industrious	Persistent
Dynamic	Energetic
Enterprising	Enthusiastic
Consistent	Organized
Professional	Methodical
Skillful	Passionate

Concepts

Answer the following questions about letters of inquiry.

1) What is the main idea of a follow-up letter?

2) What does it mean to justify the letter? Why is it a good idea?

3) Why do you begin with your own address and not your name for a follow-up letter?

4) What is the difference between the hard copy and e-mail version of a follow-up letter?

5) What information is included in the body of a follow-up letter?

11 UNIT

The Kindest Words

You're Hired!

Unit 11 The Kindest Words

- Create a thank-you letter
- Learn about the 7 Rules of Thank You
- Reinforce resume and interview vocabulary

Vocabulary

- Pleasure
- Gracious
- Expansion
- Current
- Decision
- To extend
- Occasion
- To make sense
- Gratitude
- To mention

- Especially
- Particularly
- Wise
- To support
- In the event
- Suitable
- Courteous
- To appreciate
- To acknowledge
- To detract

Let's Get Started

Conversation I

1. Listen to the conversation between the two speakers. What issue is being discussed?

Hector:	Hi, Danielle. How are you? Better yet, how did that meeting go last night?
Danielle:	It was great, really great. I arrived on time, only waited a few minutes to see Mr. Kim, and we had a great talk.
Hector:	Did you get a chance to discuss department expansion?
Danielle:	I did. He's on board. It went so well, Hector, that after the meeting Mr. Kim invited me to have dinner with him and his team.
Hector:	Wow! Danielle, that's fantastic. What a great opportunity.
Danielle:	Yes, I agree. Now I should write him a thank-you letter. A phone call just isn't enough.
Hector:	I agree. Sometimes a formal thank-you letter, or even an e-mail really shows people that you appreciate what they do for you. They can see that you have taken time from your day to thank them. It's a courteous thing to do.
Danielle:	I'll get started now, but there is just one thing.
Hector:	What's that?
Danielle:	I have never written a thank-you letter before. I am not sure where to begin.
Hector:	Let's do some research together and see what we can find. It's useful information. It won't hurt me a bit to know this stuff, either.

Hector: Hi, Danielle. How are you? (1) _____ yet, how did that meeting go last night?

Danielle: It was great, really great. I arrived on time, only (2) _____ a few minutes to see Mr. Kim, and we had a great talk.

Hector: Did you get a (3) _____ to discuss department (4) _____?

Danielle: I did. He's (5) _____. It went so well, Hector, that after the meeting Mr. Kim invited me to have dinner with he and his team.

Hector: Wow! Danielle, that's (6) _____. What a great opportunity.

Danielle: Yes, I agree. Now I should write him a (7) _____ letter. A phone call just isn't enough.

Hector: I agree. (8) _____ a formal thank-you letter, or even an e-mail really shows people that you appreciate what they do for you. They can see that you have taken time from your day to thank them. It's a (9) _____ thing to do.

Danielle: I'll get started now, but there is just one thing.

Hector: What's that?

Danielle: I have never written a thank-you letter before. I am not sure where to begin.

Hector: Let's do some research together and see what we can find. It's useful (10) _____. It won't hurt me a bit to know this stuff, either.

Conversation Ⅱ

1. Listen to the conversation between the two speakers. What information has been listed about making a great thank-you letter?

Danielle:	This web site says that I should use a formal business letter heading, with my address, phone number and even e-mail address. Then I list the date, and Mr. Kim's address.
Hector:	Right. That makes sense. How is the body of the letter different from a follow-up letter, for example?
Danielle:	It's shorter! Really, I think a thank-you letter focuses more on the simple act of thanking the person for the meeting, phone call, gift, whatever. A follow-up letter should review what happened and remind the reader why it happened. It should also plan the next step of action with the reader. It's simply a more complex letter.
Hector:	Well, let's get busy and draft you a thank-you letter.

.

2. Listen again and fill in the missing parts of speech.

Danielle: (1) _____ I should use a formal business letter heading, with my address, phone number and even e-mail address. Then I list the date, and Mr. Kim's address.

Hector: Right. (2) _____. How is the body of the letter different from a follow-up letter, for example?

Danielle: It's shorter! Really, I think a thank-you letter focuses more on the simple act of thanking the person for the meeting, phone call, gift, whatever. (3) _____ what happened and remind the reader why it happened. It should also plan the next step of action with the reader. (4) _____ more complex letter.

Hector: Well, (5) _____ and draft you a thank-you letter.

Let's Get to Business

Thank-You Letter Sample

872-9 Unhaeng-dong, Jung-gu
Daejeon, South Korea
010-1234-5678
abcde@kmail.com

February 15, 2012

Mr. Dong-ju Kim
736-4 Dunsong-dong, Seo-gu
Daejeon, South Korea

Dear Mr. Kim,

I would like to take this opportunity to thank you. It was a pleasure to meet with you. It was especially gracious of you to invite me to dine with you and your colleagues after our meeting together. I had a wonderful time and particularly enjoyed the meal.

I really agreed with your points on department expansion. I think that you are wise for taking your current position with the company. I want you to know that I support your decisions and would continue to do so in the event that a contract is signed between our two companies.

Again, Mr. Kim, it was truly a pleasure to meet with you. Thank you kindly for your time, and for the dinner invitation. I can see you truly care about the relationships you have with your colleagues.

Please extend my sincere thanks to your team. I look forward to another successful meeting in the near future.

Sincerely,

Seung-gyo Kim

Seung-gyo Kim

Thank-You Letter Template

Your address line 1
Your address line 2
Your telephone number
Your e-mail address

Date

Receiver's name
Receiver's address line 1
Receiver's address line 2

Opening phrase:

Thank the reader for the meeting, phone call, gift, etc. Be sure you mention exactly what you are thanking them for. Sometimes busy businessmen and women send many gifts, hold many meetings and make many phone calls. Be sure that they remember who you are and what they did for you. Be specific about why you enjoyed or appreciated what they did for you.

Mention a point from the meeting or phone call in the second paragraph. This will remind them that it was truly important to you and that you were listening to them. If they sent you a gift you can remark about the taste or quality.

Thank them again. If you met in a group, mention the group or some names you can remember. Extend your thanks to them, as well. If it is appropriate, mention a future meeting, etc.

Letter closing,

(signature)

Your name

Practice Makes Perfect

Write Your Own

Complete the Text

872-9 Unhaeng-dong, Jung-gu
Daejeon, South Korea
010-1234-5678
abcde@kmail.com

February 15, 2012

Mr. Dong-ju Kim
736-4 Dunsong-dong, Seo-gu
Daejeon, South Korea

Dear Mr. Kim,

I would like to take this opportunity to thank you. It was a (1) _____ to meet with you. It was (2) _____ (3) _____ of you to invite me to dine with you and your colleagues after our meeting together. I had a (4) _____ time and (5) _____ enjoyed the meal.

I really agreed with your points on department (6) _____. I think that you are (7) _____ for taking your (8) _____ (9) _____ with the (10) _____. I want you to know that I (11) _____ your (12) _____ and would continue to do so (13) _____ (14) _____ (15) _____ that a (16) _____ is signed between our two companies.

Again, Mr. Kim, it was truly a pleasure to meet with you. Thank you (17) _____ for your time, and for the dinner invitation. I can see you truly care about the (18) _____ you have with your colleagues.

Please (19) _____ my sincere thanks to your team. I look forward to (20) _____ successful meeting in the near future.

Sincerely,

Seung-gyo Kim

Seung-gyo Kim

Working with Words

The Power of Quotes

When you can't find your own words, borrow someone else's. Quotes can help you express your feelings of gratitude in a unique and creative way. Quotes can create a casual, rather than formal, atmosphere in a letter. Be sure that a quote is appropriate for the occasion, though. Here are a few ideas for thank-you quotes.

'Thank You' for Your Kindness
One can pay back the loan of gold, but one dies forever in debt to those who are kind.
[Malayan Proverb]

The smallest act of kindness is worth more than the grandest intention.
[Oscar Wilde]

Kindness is the language which the deaf can hear and the blind can see.
[Mark Twain]

How beautiful a day can be when kindness touches it!
[George Elliston]

The 7 Rules of Thank You

1. **Know when to write.**
You have an opportunity to say thank-you anytime someone has:
- Delivered good service.
- Done something extra for you.
- Been especially thoughtful, prompt, or efficient.
- Given you an opportunity (an interview, a referral, etc.).
- Given you a gift or paid for your meal.
- Been a special pleasure to work with.
- Consistently met or exceeded your expectations.

2. **Write promptly.**
Although a sincere thank-you is welcome anytime, the sooner your write the thank-you letter, the more clearly you can remember the details. It's easier to write a letter sooner, rather than later.

3. **Say "thank-you" sincerely and specifically.**

4. **Say thanks graciously and without negativity.**
Do not mention anything that will detract from your thanks and appreciation.

5. **Say thank-you warmly.**
Always use the other person's name and the personal pronouns "I" and "we". For instance, write:
"I appreciate your time", not "your time is appreciated."

6. Choose the right format; email, letter, note, or card.

Features of email:
- It is right for someone who is regularly on a computer.
- It does not stand out as special or individual.
- It is perceived as informal.
- It is quick to write, send, and forward.
- It can be any length, from one or two sentences to several paragraphs.

Features of a typed letter or memo:
- It is suitable to acknowledge a donation or contribution of money or goods.
- It fits well to thank someone for significant help or great customer service.
- It is right when the thank-you letter may end up in a personnel file.
- It must be at least two paragraphs.

Features of a handwritten card or note:
- It communicates a personal touch.
- It is the perfect response to a meal, flowers, gift, or personal assistance.
- It is short, typically from two sentences to two paragraphs.

7. Say "thank-you" without saying please.

When you say thanks, do not ask for anything. Asking detracts from your thank-you and suggests that gratitude is not the real reason for your message.

Concepts

Answer the following questions about thank-you letters.

1) How is a thank-you letter different from a follow-up letter?

2) For which occasions should you write a thank-you letter?

3) What should you never say in a thank-you letter?

4) Why is a letter or e-mail more effective than a phone call for thanking someone?

5) What are some of the features of a thank-you e-mail?

UNIT 12

Just Say No

You're Hired!

Unit **12**   Just Say No

- Create a letter of decline to turn down a job offer
- Learn about words to include and exclude
- Reinforce resume and interview vocabulary

Vocabulary

- To turn down
- To consider
- Staff (noun)
- Offer (noun)
- To deliberate
- Adaptable
- Conscientious
- Motivated
- Tactful

- To decline
- Seminar
- Grateful
- To be impressed
- Accurate
- Adept
- Diplomatic
- Objective
- To conduct

Let's Get Started

Conversation Ⅰ

1. Listen to the conversation between the two speakers. What issue is being discussed?

Derrick:	This is so great, Yumi. I never imagined that I would receive so many job offers. It was difficult, but after writing several resumes and cover letters, I finally received my dream job offer.
Yumi:	Awesome! Which offer will you take? Will you go with Greenley Corp.?
Derrick:	No. Not this time. I decided to go with a company in Busan, rather than Seoul. I should make one last contact with Greenley though. I might want to work with them in the future.
Yumi:	When you don't accept a job offer, you should always send the company a letter or e-mail of decline.
Derrick:	Yumi, I think you know everything. So, tell me more!
Yumi:	It's simple. You must thank the company for considering you for the job. Then, you tell them that you respectfully decline their offer.
Derrick:	That sounds like a great way to stay in good graces with them. Honestly, I want to stay in contact with some of these companies, just in case I need a job in the future.
Yumi:	Already planning for another job?
Derrick:	Better to be the anvil of destiny than the beast of judgment.
Yumi:	What? What in the world?
Derrick:	Nothing. What I meant to say was that it's never too early to plan, and besides that, I want to leave all of my professional experiences looking like a well-educated and respectful man.
Yumi:	You have a good point. Conducting our job search doesn't stop when we receive an offer. We should follow it through to the end.
Derrick:	Now Yumi, can you help me write this letter? I think I understand, but I want to know specifically what to write.

2. Listen again, and fill in the missing parts of speech.

Derrick: This is so great, Yumi. I never (1) _____ that I would receive so many job offers. It was difficult, but after writing several resumes and cover letters, I finally (2) _____ my dream job offer.

Yumi: (3) _____! Which offer will you take? Will you go with Greenley Corp.?

Derrick: No. Not this time. I decided to go with a company in Busan, rather than Seoul. I should make one last contact with Greenley though. I might want to work with them in the (4) _____.

Yumi: When you don't accept a job offer, you should always send the company a letter or e-mail of (5) _____.

Derrick: Yumi, I think you know (6) _____. So, tell me more!

Yumi: It's simple. You must thank the company for considering you for the job. Then, you tell them that you (7) _____ decline their offer.

Derrick: That sounds like a great way to stay in good graces with them. Honestly, I want to stay in contact with some of these companies, just in case I need a job in the future.

Yumi: Already planning for another job?

Derrick: Better to be the anvil of destiny than the beast of judgment.

Yumi: What? What in the world?

Derrick: Nothing. What I meant to say was that it's never too early to plan, and besides that, I want to leave all of my professional experiences looking like a well-educated and (8) _____ man.

Yumi: You have a good point. (9) _____ our job search doesn't stop when we receive an offer. We should follow it through to the end.

Derrick: Now Yumi, can you help me write this letter? I think I (10) _____, but I want to know specifically what to write.

Conversation Ⅱ

1. Listen to the conversation between the two speakers. What information has been listed about making a great letter of decline?

Yumi:	First, begin the letter the way you would any business letter, use the standard heading.
Derrick:	Okay. What's next?
Yumi:	Well, the first paragraph is essentially thanking the reader for the job offer. Then you should use the next and last paragraphs to decline and wish the reader continued success.
Derrick:	Great. It sounds like a short letter? Am I wrong?
Yumi:	No, you're right. It's a short, respectful letter. It's straight to the point.

Yumi: First, begin the letter the way you would any business letter.

(1) _____.

Derrick: Okay. (2) _____?

Yumi: Well, the first paragraph is essentially thanking the reader for the job offer. Then you should (3) _____ paragraphs to decline and wish the reader continued success.

Derrick: Great. It sounds like a short letter? (4) _____?

Yumi: No, you're right. It's a short, respectful letter.

(5) _____.

Let's Get to Business

....

Letter of Decline Sample

123-4 Myeong-dong, Jung-gu
Seoul, South Korea
010-1234-5678
1234@kmail.com

March 15, 2010

Mrs. Meong-hee Kim
987-4 Itewon-dong, Yeongsan-gu
Seoul, South Korea

Dear Mrs. Kim:

Thank you for the time and effort you spent considering me for a position as seminar leader. I appreciate your time and effort, as well as those of your staff. I am grateful for your offer of employment.

Because I was so impressed with Greenley Corp., I had a difficult decision to make. After much thought and careful deliberation, however, I have decided not to accept your offer.

I wish you and Greenley Corp. continued success. I hope our paths will cross again in the future.
Thank you again for your time and consideration.

Sincerely,
Derrick Lee
Derrick Lee

Letter of Decline Template

Your address line 1
Your address line 2
Your telephone number
Your e-mail address

Date

Receiver's name
Receiver's address line 1
Receiver's address line 2

Opening phrase:

Thank the reader for considering you for the job. Specifically list the company name and job title. Tell them you are grateful for the offer. Acknowledge their work and the work of their staff, if they had one.

In the second paragraph you respectfully decline the job offer. Tell the reader that you had a difficult time making a decision. You do not have to tell them why you are declining. Never say anything negative about the company or any other company in your letter. Be gracious, even if you have had a bad experience.

Thank them again. Wish them well, and tell them you hope to meet them again.

Letter closing,
(Signature)
Your name

Practice Makes Perfect

Write Your Own

Complete the Text

123-4 Myeong-dong, Jung-gu
Seoul, South Korea
010-1234-5678
1234@kmail.com

March 15, 2010

Mrs. Meong-hee Kim
987-4 Itewon-dong, Yeongsan-gu
Seoul, South Korea

Dear Mrs. Kim:

Thank you for the time and effort you spent (1) _____ me for a position as (2) _____ leader. I appreciate your time and effort, as well as those of your (3) _____. I am (4) _____ for your (5) _____ _____ of employment.

Because I was so (6) _____ with Greenley Corp., I had a difficult (7) _____ to make. After much thought and careful (8) _____ _____, however, I have decided not to accept your offer.

I (9) _____ you and Greenley Corp. (10) _____ success. I hope our (11) _____ will cross again in the future.
Thank you again for your time and consideration.

(12) _____,
Derrick Lee
Derrick Lee

Working with Words

The Good, the Bad, and the Misspelled

Powerwords will strengthen your resume. Grammar errors, and misspelled words will weaken it. The following is a list of words to avoid in your resume.

- **Abbreviations**: Assume the reader prefers to read whole words. Assume they do not understand your abbreviations.
- **Acronyms**: If you must use them for your field, use them sparingly.
- **Personal pronouns**: Leave out I, me and my.
- **Negative words**: Bored, fired, hate, angry, look bad: There is no way to use these words successfully in a resume.
- **Any word you can't define**: If you need to get a dictionary out to define your own resume, skip the word and pick another that you are more familiar with. Using big words does not make you look smarter.
- **Trendy words, buzzwords**: Over-use of popular terms can date your resume or make you seem less professional.

The following is a list of adjectives that help strengthen your resume.

Accurate	Adaptable
Adept	Conscientious
Diplomatic	Innovative
Motivated	Objective
Productive	Tactful

Concepts

Answer the following questions about letters of inquiry.

1) Why is writing a letter of decline important?

2) What are the primary contents of a letter of decline?

3) Why should you avoid trendy words in your resume?

4) Which powerwords from chapter 12 best describe you? Why do you think so?

5) Why should you avoid using words you cannot describe?

REFERENCES

Career Services. 18 December 2009. <http://www.career.vt.edu>.
JobBank USA. 12 January 2010. <http://www.jobbankusa.com>.
Klemsen, Katie Mae. "The SEEK Approach." 2006.
Syntax Training. 04 January 2010.
<http://www.syntaxtraining.com/>

·저/자/소/개·

Myeong-hee Seong

　Ph.D., Korea University

　Professor, Eulji University

Katie Mae Klemsen

　MA, Monterey Institute of International Studies

　Professor, Eulji University

You're Hired!
Resume & Letter Writing for English Language Learners

2010년　2월 20일　인 쇄
2010년　2월 25일　발 행

저 자　　Myeong-hee Seong
　　　　　Katie Mae Klemsen

발행인　(寅製) 진　욱　상

발행처　🔖 백산출판사
서울시 성북구 정릉3동 653-40
　등록 : 1974. 1. 9. 제 1-72호
　전화 : 914-1621, 917-6240
　FAX : 912-4438
http://www.baek-san.com
edit@baek-san.com

저자와
합의하에
인지첩부
생략

값 13,000 원(CD포함)
ISBN 978-89-6183-285-4(93740)